D1120599

THE GREAT CONVERSATION

A HISTORICAL INTRODUCTION TO PHILOSOPHY

Third Edition

Norman Melchert

Virginia Commonwealth University

Mayfield Publishing Company
Mountain View, California
London • Toronto

International Standard Book Number: 0-7674-0021-6

Manufactured in the United States of America
10 9 8 7 6 5 4 3 2 1

Mayfield Publishing Company
1280 Villa Street
Mountain View, California 94041

CONTENTS

PREFACE

This Instructor's Manual accompanies the third edition of The Great Conversation. I had been reluctant to do a manual of this sort for several reasons. For one thing, the text is designed for beginning students in philosophy—freshmen and sophomores, primarily—and it was hard for me to believe it couldn't be taught well by professionals without such help. For another, I was sure that many users of the text were excellent teachers who could doubtless teach me a thing or two about how to use the book.

But I was persuaded that it would be useful to the especially harried instructors among us, and might even enrich somewhat the teaching of the very best. In no case do I imagine that an instructor will rely solely on the materials in this little manual. What you have here is supplementary stuff—some suggestions that may be an aid to doing a bit better what you no doubt do well even now.

I would be grateful for reactions to the manual, and for suggestions about improvement. To that end, I offer here my e-mail address: <npmelche@titan.vcu.edu>.

Here let me make some general comments about how I teach The Great Conversation. I'm sure there are many good ways to do it, and I'd be happy to hear about what has worked for you.

1. I have taught it as both a full-year course and as a one-semester course, using one of the paperback volumes. Descartes gets taught in both terms.

2. Classes are—as is appropriate for this particular text—intensely interactive. To make this work, students must have read the assignment ahead of time, so I make a big point of the importance of this. I make sure to learn the students' names (at least in classes smaller than fifty). Asking them to always sit in the same place—their choice, but always the same place—helps in this regard. It sometimes takes a few weeks before they get the idea that discussion will predominate in class, but eventually the classes are very lively.

3. To break the material into chunks students can master, I usually give five short quizzes during the term. Dates for the quizzes are announced in the syllabus. They occupy the first fifteen minutes of a class period. The best four of these are counted toward the grade, and I do not offer make-ups on quizzes unless a student misses more than one, in which case the make-up is an oral quiz in my office.

4. My practice has been to use short-answer questions in the quizzes, for the most part. I find these more satisfactory than multiple-choice questions for finding out if students actually understand the material. Grading five short answers (out of a choice of seven or eight) doesn't take that long for forty students. When I have had much larger classes, the department has hired as graders previous students who did well in the class. With model answers before them, and I available for questions, these students do quite a good job. And they enjoy it.

5. I always give back model answers to quiz questions when I return the quizzes—nearly always in the next class period. This allows students to compare their answers with good answers; is educationally sound, I think; and removes the need to go over the quizzes in class. It also has the side-benefit of reducing arguments about the scoring virtually to zero. It does mean that quizzes cannot be used over and over again one semester after another. But that seems a small price to pay for the benefits.

6. Typically there is also a mid-term and a comprehensive final exam. These always include one or two essay questions (some choice allowed), typically of a comparative nature. I also give back model answers for the mid-term.

7. A paper (occasionally two papers) is assigned that has a quite different aim from that of the quizzes and exams. In the paper, students are to philosophize, not report their understanding of someone else's philosophizing. Some sample paper assignments are included at the end of this manual.

Well, that's how I do it. Because I seldom use multiple-choice questions, and I know they are tricky to write, you may find problems with the questions in the manual. If you do, I'd appreciate hearing about them. Perhaps a future printing can do better.

CHAPTER 1
BEFORE PHILOSOPHY
Myth in Hesiod and Homer

ESSENTIAL POINTS

- Myth as stories, typically about beginnings and the gods
- Hesiod: War Among the Gods
  * Hesiod claims inspiration from the muses
  * The origins of all things from chaos
  * The Titans, overthrown by Zeus and his allies
  * The (relative) orderliness of the Olympians and their rule over the universe
- Homer: Heroes, Gods, and Excellence
  * The war against Troy
    — The anger of Achilles
    — Its terrible consequences
  * Moderation the chief virtue
  * Justice as each getting his due; the quest for honor
  * The role of the gods
  * Mortals are not gods; Hubris

TEACHING SUGGESTIONS

1. There is plenty of occult stuff around these days to convince students the quarrel between philosophy and myth is not over. Hesiod may seem arcane, but it should not be hard to get them to see that the reasons for accepting Hesiod are about the same as the reasons many widely popular schemes are accepted today. For clues to some examples, you might take a look at Martin Gardner's *The New Age: Notes of a Fringe Watcher*, Prometheus Books, 1988.

2. There should be enough in the chapter to get students to appreciate the dramatic and wonderful story of *The Iliad*—maybe even to persuade some of them to read it. The morals drawn by Homer will reverberate through Greek philosophy.

EXAM QUESTIONS
A. Multiple-Choice Questions

1. Hesiod claimed to write his poems
    a. after exhaustive study of the heavens and the earth.
    b. by collecting stories that had been passed down from the ancestors.
    x c. through divine inspiration.
    d. because he was bored while herding sheep on holy Helicon.

2. Zeus came to be "father of gods and men," according to Hesiod,
    a. by swallowing a stone and vomiting it up again.
    x b. through war against his father.
    c. by general acclamation of all the other gods.
    d. because he was the first-born son of Earth and Heaven.

3. The quarrel between Achilles and Agamemnon began when
    x a. Agamemnon demanded that Achilles give him the woman Achilles had been awarded as spoils from a battle.
    b. Hector killed Achilles' friend, Patroclus.
    c. Achilles wanted the woman Agamemnon had been awarded as spoils from a battle.
    d. Apollo sent a plague on the army.

4. The gods, in Homer's poem,
    a. urge men to be more like themselves.
    b. live in delight and splendor on Olympus, scarcely ever thinking about the affairs of men.
    c. function as moral ideals for human beings, who have a hard time living up to the gods' standards.
    x d. care about the honor given them by men.

5. Homer
    a. advises humans to live well, so as to merit eternal life.
    x b. praises moderation.
    c. disparages the quest for honor and glory, since it leads to quarrels and disaster for so many.
    d. portrays gods and men as immortal.

2

B. Short-Answer Questions

1. How, according to Hesiod, did Zeus come to be king of the gods?

He was born of Rhea and Kronos, both Titans, together with numerous brothers and sisters. Kronos, jealous of his power, was swallowing each of his children after birth, but Rhea hid Zeus and gave Kronos a stone to swallow instead. When he grew up, Zeus freed his siblings and together with some allies waged war on the Titans, dethroning them and becoming ruler himself.

2. What brought on the quarrel between Agamemnon and Achilles?

The daughter of a priest of Apollo had been captured in a raid on a Trojan ally and had been awarded to Agamemnon. He refused to return her to her father when ransom was offered. Apollo sent a plague to teach them to honor the god; to rid the army of the plague, Agamemnon gave back the girl. He demanded in return, however, the woman of Achilles. And Achilles was furious.

3. How does The Iliad end?

After Achilles' friend Patroclus is killed by Hector, Achilles re-enters the battle. In single combat, he kills Hector and drags his body behind his chariot back to his tent. At night, disguised, Hector's father, King Priam sneaks through the Greek lines, goes to Achilles, and begs for the body of his son. Achilles and Priam weep together, and Achilles gives him what he wants.

4. What virtues are praised in The Iliad?

Courage, cleverness, physical prowess, and moderation—the latter because it was the lack of moderation in Achilles' anger that brought near destruction to the Greeks.

5. Describe the gods of Olympus as Homer portrays them.

They are powerful, jealous of the honor due them, and interested in the affairs of men, about which they often take sides and quarrel among themselves. They form a kind of family, many of them being related to one another. They are the immortals, and as such enjoy a kind of happiness denied to mortals. Zeus is king among them and the most powerful, though he is not all powerful.

C. Essay Questions

1.   What can we learn about how to be excellent human beings from Homer's poem?

2.   What does the term "theogony" mean? Relate several of the central events of Hesiod's theogony.

CHAPTER 2
PHILOSOPHY BEFORE SOCRATES

ESSENTIAL POINTS

- Basic problems of early philosophy
  * The one and the many
  * Reality and appearance
  * The place of humans in the universe
- Thales: The One as Water
  * Looking to this world for explanations
    — Water as the cause and element of all things
    — All things are filled with gods
- Anaximander: The One as the Boundless
  * Problems with Thales' hypothesis
  * The argument for the Boundless
  * Differentiation through a vortex motion
  * Things make reparation to each other for injustice
- Xenophanes: The Gods as Fictions
  * The gods are immoral
  * The gods are made in the image of mortals
  * One god, not similar to mortals
  * Humans' relation to the truth
- Heraclitus: Oneness in the *Logos*
  * All things are in flux and in opposition
  * The world-order, fire, the *logos*
  * Wisdom is understanding the *logos*
  * Learning through sight, hearing, understanding
  * Happiness and moderation: internal opposition is essential
- Parmenides: Only the One
  * The premises of his argument: thought and being are the same; nothing is not; nothing cannot be thought
  * The conclusions
    — There is not a many
    — There can be no change
    — Even time must be an illusion
  * Characteristics of the One
  * Rationalism

- Zeno: The Paradoxes of Common Sense
  * How Zeno means to pay back Parmenides' critics "with interest"
  * Three sample arguments
  * The structure of these arguments: *reductio ad absurdum*
- Atomism: The One and the Many Reconciled
  * The Key: An Ambiguity
    — Critique of Parmenides' argument
  * The World
    — Explaining phenomena in terms of atoms and the void: light and heavy, soft and hard, flexible and rigid, change
    — Mechanism and the problem for free will
  * The Soul
    — The soul is material, too
    — Mental phenomena explained: sensations
    — We are cut off from the real by the nature of sensation, but we can reason to it
  * How to Live

TEACHING SUGGESTIONS

1. It is important that this chapter not be taught as just one view after another. I try to stress how each subsequent thinker sees a problem in a previous one and tries to solve it. Karl Popper cited these pre-Socratics as displaying the method (which he favored) of "conjectures and refutations," and that seems a promising hook on which to hang the discussions.

2. In teaching Parmenides, I have found it best to start with his conclusions: There are not many things, and nothing ever changes. These are startling enough that students wonder why anyone would ever believe such things, and they are engaged.

6

EXAM QUESTIONS
A. Multiple-Choice Questions

1. In saying that all things are full of gods, Thales apparently meant that
    a. Homer was right in saying that what happens can be attributed to the will of the gods.
    b. traditional religious views could be defended after all.
  x c. explanations of events in the world could be explained in terms of events in the world.
    d. science has its limits.

2. Anaximander's argument for the Boundless as that out of which all things come
    a. appeals to the infinite quality of the universe.
  x b. assumes that observable features of the world all need explaining.
    c. holds that explanations can go back and back infinitely far.
    d. identifies the Boundless with the gods of Homer's poems.

3. How does Anaximander explain the generation of the many things in our experience?
  x a. By positing a cosmic swirl or vortex that spins like things to like.
    b. By a theory of evolution.
    c. By an appeal to one god, unlike us in any way.
    d. By an infinite regress argument.

4. Xenophanes criticizes the Homeric gods
    a. for not coming to our aid when we need them.
  x b. as unworthy of our admiration and respect.
    c. and says there are no gods at all.
    d. and substitutes other gods from more moral traditions.

5. Xenophanes says that with respect to the truth,
   a. humans have never known it and will never know it.
   b. it was revealed to us from of old.
   x c. even if we knew it, we couldn't know for sure that we knew it.
   d. if we seek it, not relying on the stories of the poets, we will be sure to find it.

6. What, according to Heraclitus, is wisdom?
   a. Minding your own business and being content with what you have.
   b. Satisfying your every desire.
   c. Recognizing that life in this world is but a dream.
   x d. Understanding the thought that steers all things.

7. Most people, Heraclitus says,
   a. but not all, are in daily contact with the *logos*.
   x b. live as though their thought were private to themselves.
   c. are willing and unwilling to be called Zeus.
   d. fight against impulse, for what it wants it buys at the expense of the soul.

8. Parmenides is rightly called a rationalist because
   a. he rationalizes and deceives himself about the truth.
   b. he gives reasons explaining all things, even change.
   c. unlike his predecessors, he was a rational person.
   x d. he is willing to follow the argument wherever it leads.

9. The One of Parmenides is
   a. in continual flux and opposition.
   x b. unchanging, all alike, and eternal.
   c. identical in concept with the Boundless of Anaximander, which spins the many out of its own substance.
   d. a useful fiction, Parmenides says, that provides a unity to the many diverse things in the universe.

10. Democritus says that sweet and bitter exist by convention. By this he means that
    a. if we came to agree they didn't exist, they would disappear.
    b. the words "sweet" and "bitter" (or their Greek equivalents) were agreed to by humans at a convention in Athens.
    x c. their nature depends as much on us as on the things themselves.
    d. convention is an avenue into the real.

B. Short-Answer Questions

1. In what way is Thales' statement that water is the origin and element of all things a criticism of the Homeric tradition?
    Homer tended to explain things in terms of the will of the gods. For instance, the plague that fell on Agamemnon's army was caused by an angry Apollo. Thales, in contrast, holds that events in the world have an explanation in terms of some perfectly natural, worldly, cause—water and its variants. If Thales is right, then Homer must be wrong.

2. What does Thales mean when he says that all things are filled with gods?
    He means that we do not have to look beyond things to find the explanations for their behavior. Gods were understood as the movers, those who made things happen. And Thales says that the principles that account for the qualities of things and for their action, change, and movement are immortal and are resident in the things themselves.

3. What is Anaximander's argument for his belief that it cannot be water that is the final explanation of all things, but something Boundless?
    Since water is just one of the many things we experience, it too needs explanation. If water originates in something else, call it A, then A also requires explaining. Suppose A is explained by B. But B calls for explanation as well. Then B must originate in C—and so on and on. But this regress cannot go on to infinity. So there must be something not requiring an origin, something that is an origin but doesn't *have* an origin. This must be something without beginning or ending, something limitless, infinite, or Boundless.

4. What is Anaximander's explanation of how the many things of our experience emerge from the Boundless?

The Boundless is swirling in a great vortex motion. What happens in such a swirl is that things tend to cluster with things like themselves, and the heavier they are, the closer to the center of the swirl they come. So the cold and heavy earth is deposited at the center, a very hot and fiery sphere of fire is at the periphery, with water and air between. More specific changes occur because of the interactions among these basic elements.

5. State Xenophanes' two criticisms of the Homeric gods.

(1) Homer portrays the gods as doing shameful things. (2) Since different images of gods are found in different cultures, it is evident that they are fictions, invented by the people of some particular culture.

6. How—and how not—according to Xenophanes, are we to learn the truth.

Xenophanes says that the truth has not been revealed to us by the gods, so we have to seek for it. He adds that our aim should be to make our opinions more and more like the truth, since we can never be certain that we do have it—even when we do.

7. How does Heraclitus use the concept of the logos to solve the problem of the One and the Many?

Why is this world of many things not just a chaos, but one world, a universe? Because there is a rational structure or pattern in which everything has its proper place. This structure is the *logos*, which makes One out of Many; it does not come into being or pass away; it is divine.

8. Explain Heraclitus' saying that "War is father and king of all."

By "war" Heraclitus means opposition, which is essential to the nature of each thing. Everything is a unity or harmony of elements in tension with one another—the river, the lyre, a just society. If one aspect or force were to gain the upper hand, there would be no distinct things at all. So war is "father" of all in that it brings things into being, and "king" of all in that it rules over their existence as long as they last.

9. What is Parmenides' argument that there cannot be any change in reality?

If there were change, it would involve a transition from what is not to what is, or from what is to what is not. When water is brought to the boil, for instance, it leaves the state of not boiling and moves to the state where it is boiling. But what is not cannot be thought, and not being cannot be. So, despite the testimony of our senses, in reality there cannot be any change. There is only the One, eternal, immutable, indivisible.

10. What is Parmenides' argument that there cannot be many things in reality?

Whatever is, is. If there were many things, what could separate one thing that is from another that is? Only what is not. But what is not is not, and cannot be thought. So it is impossible that one thing be separated from another, so there cannot be, nor be thought to be, many things.

11. Sketch Zeno's paradox of the arrow and explain why he thought it paid back Parmenides' critics "with interest."

If an arrow moves, it must either move in the space it occupies or in a space it does not occupy. It can do neither, so it cannot move. Zeno thought this argument showed that common sense beliefs were contradictory, since common sense holds that the arrow does move, and from common sense premises it can be deduced that it does not move. So common sense was not only false, but necessarily false.

12. Sketch the argument of the atomists—Democritus, for instance—that they claim undermines Parmenides' proof that there cannot be many things.

The atomists claim to find an ambiguity in the proof of Parmenides. He argues that nothing is not, and in one sense that is correct, but in another it is not. It is correct for absolutely nothing, or nothing at all; but in the sense of No-thing—that is, no body—it can perfectly well exist. As such, it is the void, or empty space, which can separate one thing from another and make possible the existence of many things.

13. What, according to Democritus, explains the great variety of things in the world?

The things that we are familiar with are all composed of atoms, those tiny indissoluble, eternal bits that differ from each other in shape, size, and position. Atoms hook into each other in a great variety of ways, thus constituting soft things and hard, large things and small, etc. When they lose their connections, the things we know pass away, though the atoms of which they are composed do not.

14. What problem does Democritus' atomism raise for free choice?

If atomism is true, then everything that exists is made up of atoms and the void—including human beings. Atoms interact in a purely mechanical fashion, without any purpose or intention. So what happens is a strict consequence of the laws of motion and the prior state of things. And this applies to our choices, too. So if atomism is correct, it is a kind of illusion that we initiate actions; all our choices are but a necessary result of a prior state of the world. This view is called "determinism."

C. Essay Questions

1. Sum up Heraclitus' solution to the problem of the One and the Many.

2. Heraclitus says, "Wisdom is one thing: to understand the thought which steers all things through all things." Explain.

3. On atomist principles, what happens to the notion of a cosmic intelligence (a god)? And why?

4. How does Parmenides resolve the problem of reality and appearance? Why does it turn out the way it does?

5. Write a dialogue in which a Parmenidean and an atomist debate about the nature of reality.

CHAPTER 3
THE SOPHISTS
Rhetoric and Relativism in Athens

ESSENTIAL POINTS

- Democracy
- The Persian Wars
    * Marathon in 490 B.C.
    * Thermopylae and Salamis in 480 B.C.
    * The Athenian Empire
    * Pericles on the glory of Athens
- The Sophists
    * Modern education for democratic Athens
    * Rhetoric
        — The principles and the practice of persuasive speaking
        — Techniques for teaching
        — Making the weaker argument into the stronger
        — Skeptical implications
    * Relativism
        — Protagoras: man the measure
        — The impact of acquaintance with other cultures
    * *Physis* and *Nomos*
        — How to make the distinction
        — Applying the distinction: to the gods, to justice
        — Is there a justice distinct from convention?
            † Heraclitus and Sophocles: yes
            † Antiphon: yes, but natural justice is antithetical to human law
            † The victory goes to the best speaker
        — Callicles on the origin of conventional justice
- Athens and Sparta at War
    * Internal struggles in Athens
    * Moderation abandoned
    * Euripides' *Hippolytus* and the influence of rhetoric
- Aristophanes and Reaction
    * Socrates as portrayed in *The Clouds*
    * The story, and what Pheidippides learns
    * The question posed: Is it always only a question of who

TEACHING SUGGESTIONS

Many students find in the Sophists an early anticipation of views they strongly hold—usually without having examined them. So the issue between the Sophists and Socrates is a live one for them. In teaching this chapter I do not raise critical questions about rhetoric or relativism (though Euripides and Aristophanes do), but I try to make sure they see the point of the question at the end.

EXAM QUESTIONS
A. Multiple-Choice Questions

1. On which point does Pericles *not* express pride in Athens?
    a. The government of Athens is a model for neighboring city-states to copy.
    b. Athenians obey their laws.
    c. Athenians love what is beautiful without becoming soft.
    x d. Athens has conquered most of the known world.

2. What does Protagoras promise to teach Hippocrates?
    x a. Good planning, so that he can run his own estate and contribute to the welfare of the city.
    b. Cleverness in speaking, so that he can avoid paying his debts.
    c. Geometry, astronomy, and flute playing.
    d. The traditional Greek virtues, exemplified in the works of Homer, the poet.

3. The key idea in rhetoric is that
    a. one should speak the truth, no matter how it affects one's interests.
    x b. one should be able to make a persuasive case for any position.
    c. with its help, one can avoid sleepwalking through life and align oneself with the *logos*.
    d. no one should take advantage of another because of rhetorical skill.

4. When Protagoras says that man is the measure of all things, he means that
   a. it is only man, of all the animals, that has devised measures for distance, weight, temperature, etc.
   b. what exists must be measured by what all men have in common.
   x c. there is no objective criterion available to humans by which to judge truth and goodness.
   d. measuring is important to man for building all sorts of things.

5. When Herodotus quotes Pindar's saying that custom is king over all, he means that
   x a. each group thinks its own native religion and culture to be the best.
   b. people would never question their own customs, which rule supreme in their habits and actions.
   c. relativism is a mistake.
   d. the king decides what customs his people should adopt.

6. The relation between *nomos* and *physis* is that
   a. the former indicates what is true by nature and the latter does not.
   b. nothing true by *nomos* could contradict anything true by *physis*.
   x c. we can change the former, but not the latter.
   d. *nomos* is divine, *physis* is human.

7. Antiphon argues that
   a. most of the things that are just by law (in the sense of *physis*) are hostile to nature.
   b. it is better to suffer injustice than to do injustice.
   c. if you break the rules of society for some advantage to yourself, it is only just (by *physis*) that you be punished.
   x d. in any case, victory goes to the best speaker.

15

8. In his comic play, *The Clouds,* Aristophanes portrays Socrates as
    a. a critic of the Sophists.
    b. the one who burns down the Thinkery.
    c. the father of Pheidippides, who wants him to learn how to make the weaker argument into the stronger.
  x d. someone who teaches for pay.

9. Which of the following is *not* a theme expressed in Euripides' play, *Hippolytus*?
    a. Rhetoric corrupts virtue.
    b. Humans are merely pawns in the hands of powers that care nothing for them.
  x c. Nothing can harm the truly innocent.
    d. Fortune is ever veering and nothing can be relied upon.

B. Short-Answer Questions

1. What did the Sophists claim to teach their students?
    They claimed to teach *arete,* excellence. They promised to instruct students in all those skills and arts that would make them successful in their city and in their private affairs.

2. What does Protagoras mean when he says that "Of all things the measure is man..."?
    A "measure" is a standard or criterion to judge by. In saying that man is the measure, Protagoras is denying that there is any objective point of view from which we can "measure" our opinions for truth. All we have is how things seem to one person or culture, to another person or culture, and so on. If things seem one way to this person and another way to that person, that may be the end of the matter—unless one can rhetorically persuade the other to change his or her mind. Taking Protagoras seriously lands one in relativism.

3. What does Protagoras say about belief in the gods?
    He expresses an agnostic point of view, saying that the subject is difficult and human life is short. He says he doesn't know, and isn't in a position to know, whether there are gods nor what they are like if they exist.

4. What is rhetoric? And what consequence does it seem to have for our ability to know the truth?

Rhetoric is the art and practice of persuasive speaking. If a rhetorically convincing case can be made for just about anything, then how can we ever tell what is true? It looks like rhetorical skill may land us in skepticism.

5. The *Sophists* claim that rhetorical skills allow a person to "make the weaker argument into the stronger." What does that mean?

A weak argument is one that doesn't have much going for it, one that is not likely to persuade if it is presented bare. Turning it into a stronger argument means transforming it so that it does persuade. A strong argument, according to the Sophists, is simply a winning argument, one that succeeds in convincing the hearer. Rhetorical skills can turn the one into the other.

6. Explain the difference between *nomos* and *physis*, offering an example of each (different from any example discussed in the text or in class).

Whatever is a matter of *nomos* depends on convention or agreement for its reality. It is true that you can't get credit toward graduation for this course unless you pay your tuition. But that is true because of the institutional arrangements in our society, and this might be changed. On the other hand, it is a matter of *physis* that if you cross the street carelessly and are struck by a car traveling 30 mph you will be injured. Nothing we could agree on could alter that connection.

7. Contrast Heraclitus and Sophocles' character Antigone, on the one hand, with Antiphon the Sophist, on the other hand, about the existence and character of natural justice.

Heraclitus says there is a natural justice (by *physis*) that expresses the *logos* and governs what ought to happen among humans. Human law, when it is doing its job, he says, is nurtured by and reflects this justice. Antigone agrees and appeals to the unwritten laws of justice against an unjust decree of the king.

Antiphon also thinks there is a natural justice, but it is not the friend of conventional law—it is its enemy. The basic law of natural justice is self-preservation, and if you violate *nomos* in order to preserve or further your life, you do nothing naturally unjust.

8. Characterize Socrates as he is portrayed in Aristophanes' comic play, *The Clouds*.

Socrates is portrayed as a Sophist, hanging in a basket studying things in the heavens as the play opens. He runs a school called the Thinkery and

17

accepts students for pay. He promises to teach students how to make the weaker argument into the stronger, and is a thorough rascal.

9. What is Callicles' theory about the origin of laws of justice in society?

It is the weak who band together to frame the laws of justice. They write them to their own advantage, of course, in order to keep the strong from dominating over them. Trying to bring everyone down to their own level, they preach equality, and call it wrong and shameful and unjust if anyone seeks an advantage over the weak. Callicles, however, thinks that true justice is exemplified by the strong taking whatever they can take.

C. Essay Questions

1. How is the practice of rhetoric, as taught by the Sophists, related to philosophical relativism and skepticism?

2. Compare Heraclitus, who says that we are all in daily contact with the *logos*—though most of us live in private worlds of our own—with Protagoras, who says that of all things, man is the measure.

3. Is it more important to be just or to appear just? In answering this question, be sure to indicate clearly whether and when you mean to be speaking of a justice by *physis* and when of a justice by *nomos*.

CHAPTER 4
SOCRATES
To Know Oneself

ESSENTIAL POINTS

- Socrates wrote nothing; Plato our main source
- Character
  * Midwifery
  * Ugliness, humor, soldiery, intensity, poverty, moderation
- Is Socrates a Sophist?
  * Some similarities: same circles, same interests
  * Some dissimilarities: takes no pay; not a teacher; searches for truth, not victory
  * Dialectic as helpful antagonism
  * Being the same kind of man as Socrates is
- What Socrates "Knows"
  * Certain things have "stood fast" for him
  * We Ought to Search for Truth
  * Human Excellence Is Knowledge
    — What sort of knowledge? *Techne*
    — Is it teachable?
  * All Wrongdoing Is Due to Ignorance
    — The importance of moral education
    — Euripides: another view
  * The Most Important Thing of All Is to Care for Your Soul
    — Better to suffer injustice than to do it
    — A good person cannot be harmed

TEACHING SUGGESTIONS

This is an easy chapter to teach, as students are generally fascinated by Socrates. They find him an attractive figure, but also puzzling and somewhat alien—as Socrates' contemporaries also did, no doubt. I try to emphasize how differently Socrates looks at things—sort of upside down and inside out. Taking Socrates seriously could change their lives.

EXAM QUESTIONS
A. Multiple-Choice Questions

1. According to the testimony of Alcibiades,
   a. Socrates was often drunk but acted courageously nonetheless.
   x b. Socrates once stood outside all day and all night thinking.
   c. the arguments of Socrates about pack asses and blacksmiths and tanners are simply laughable.
   d. Socrates was wise in that he bundled up well in the freezing cold.

2. In discussions with others, Socrates
   a. held that victory would go to the best speaker.
   b. used the arts of rhetoric as taught by the Sophists.
   c. asked questions but would answer none.
   x d. was happy to be refuted.

3. In his conversations, Socrates
   x a. often professed ignorance of the subject being discussed.
   b. tried to teach others the truth as he saw it.
   c. confessed that if an opinion seemed true to you, then that settled the matter—for you.
   d. tried not to antagonize people.

4. One of Socrates' settled convictions is that
   a. it is useless to search for the truth, for that is for the gods alone to know.
   x b. someone who knows what justice is will be just.
   c. when a person does evil, it is because his or her will is corrupt.
   d. the most important thing is to take care of your family.

5. Socrates is unlike the Sophists in that
   a. he took very little pay for his teaching, and as a result remained poor, while they grew rich.
   b. he was interested in the question of human excellence.
   c. the youth of Athens sought out his company.
   x d. he thought winning was not the main thing.

B. Short-Answer Questions

1. Alcibiades says of Socrates, "He is absolutely unique; there's no one like him...." Give a brief description of Socrates that might justify this judgment.

Having been a tough and courageous soldier, he walked about barefoot in winter, and spent whole days and nights standing still, thinking about a problem. He could drink his companions under the table but has never been seen drunk. Ugly and poor, he is moderate almost to a fault, requiring little in the way of material goods. He refrains from the homosexual relations with young men that were common in the upper classes in Athens at the time. He spends his days in the public square, talking to anyone who is interested—mostly asking them questions. His arguments seem poor things, Alcibiades says, about tailors and horse traders, but once you get inside them, he says, you see there are no others to compare. Socrates thinks he has been set in Athens by "the god" to urge his fellow citizens to virtue.

2. What kind of person must you be to benefit from a conversation with Socrates?

Socrates says that you have to be the kind of person he himself is. You need to be just as happy to be shown you are mistaken as to show that someone else is wrong. Why? Because it is a great evil to hold false opinions, and one should be grateful when another person delivers one from such an evil. In short, you must not be interested in winning, but in the truth.

3. Give two reasons for thinking of Socrates as a Sophist. And two for thinking he is not a Sophist.

Socrates is like the Sophists in being concerned about the same things—primarily human excellence. He is also like them in that he moves in the same circles and discusses things constantly with them. He is unlike the Sophists in not teaching for pay and in being concerned not with winning, but with the truth.

4. Explain the connection between (a) Socrates' practice of asking questions, (b) his characterization of himself as a midwife, and (c) his concern for the truth.

Socrates does not lecture or preach; he asks questions. The aim is to help others give birth to the ideas within themselves—as a midwife helps women give birth—and then determine whether those ideas are true—as a midwife used to determine whether the baby was legitimate. The procedure involves examining idea after idea, discarding those seen to be faulty, thus moving closer and closer to opinions that are, as Xenophanes says, "like" the truth.

5. What does it mean that human excellence is knowledge?

It means that human beings always act according to the best that they know. No one ever, Socrates thinks, does what he or she thinks is bad. It follows that if we could know what virtue or excellence is—in the way a carpenter knows what a good table is—we would be excellent persons. So it is most important not to have false opinions.

C. Essay Questions

1. Contrast, in as many ways as you can, Socrates with the Sophists.

2. Heraclitus says that "though the *logos* is common to all, the many live as though their thought were private to themselves." What might Socrates have thought about this? And how might it be connected with his questioning?

CHAPTER 5
THE TRIAL AND DEATH OF SOCRATES

ESSENTIAL POINTS

- *Euthyphro*
  - Why Socrates is at court
  - The charges against Socrates
    - Not believing in the city's gods but introducing others
    - Corrupting the youth
  - Why Euthyphro is at court
  - Socrates' "sign"
  - The question: What is piety?
    - Why Socrates thinks Euthyphro might be able to answer it
    - Why he needs an answer
    - What a good answer would provide
  - The first attempt
    - Prosecuting the wrongdoer
    - Not the right kind of answer
  - The second attempt
    - What is dear to the gods
    - Euthyphro admits that the gods quarrel
    - It follows that the same thing will be pious and impious
  - The third attempt
    - What all the gods love
    - Whether the gods love what is pious because it is pious, or it is pious because they love it
    - The third answer gives only an external characteristic of the pious; it doesn't tell us what it is
  - The fourth attempt
    - The pious is part of the just
    - Service to the gods
    - Prayer and sacrifice
    - That is what they love
    - Back to the third answer
  - Euthyphro flees

23

- *Apology*
    - Socrates draws a line from the start between himself and his accusers
    - The earlier accusers
        - What do they say?
            - † That he investigates things in the heavens and under the earth
            - † That he makes the weaker argument into the stronger
            - † That he teaches these things to others for pay
        - Socrates' replies
        - The story of the Oracle at Delphi and how he came to take up his profession
        - Questioning the politicians, the poets, and the craftsmen
        - Human wisdom
    - The later accusers
        - Who corrupts and who improves?
        - Does Socrates corrupt willingly or unwillingly?
        - Does Socrates not believe in the gods at all?
    - Could Socrates stop philosophizing in exchange for his life
    - If they kill him, they will harm themselves more than they harm him
    - Socrates is no respecter of political parties
    - No one's teacher
    - No appeal to pity
    - The verdict
        - Socrates proposes a penalty
        - Feeling happy and being happy
    - The sentence
        - Wickedness more difficult to avoid than death
        - Why death must not be an evil
- *Crito*
    - Socrates about to be executed
    - Crito argues that Socrates should escape
    - Examination of whether that would be right
    - Listening to the wise, not to just anyone
    - The health of the soul is most important

* The argument
* Socrates refuses to escape
• *Phaedo* (Death Scene)

TEACHING SUGGESTIONS

1. In teaching these dialogues, I try to stay close to the text, while engaging the students in questions and answers. There is a lot in them, and students need help seeing what some of it means. It doesn't seem appropriate to lecture on Socrates.

2. I give students outlines of both *Euthyphro* and *Apology* to help them see the structure of each.

EXAM QUESTIONS
A. Multiple-Choice Questions

1. Euthyphro meets Socrates before the court because
   a. he is being prosecuted for the murder of his father.
   x b. he is prosecuting his father for murder.
   c. he has charged Socrates with impiety.
   d. his reputation as an expert on piety has been challenged, and he is in court to defend it.

2. Socrates describes Meletus as
   a. an older man who is arrogant and meddlesome.
   b. someone well-known to himself.
   x c. a person who knows what is most important—caring that young people be well brought up.
   d. someone who couldn't be very wise, since he is bringing Socrates to court.

3. The main thing Socrates wants Euthyphro to teach him is
   a. why it is just to prosecute your father for murder.
   b. why the gods quarrel.
   x c. what makes something pious.
   d. the form of justice.

4. Examination of Euthyphro's second proposal, that the pious is what the gods love, reveals

   x a. that Euthyphro's stories about the gods lead him, together with this definition, into contradiction.

      b. that there are gods who don't agree.

      c. that we don't know what the gods love.

      d. that it only tells us how the gods regard the pious, not what it is.

5. The problem with defining piety as what all the gods love is that

      a. they don't all love the same things.

   x b. it gives only an external characteristic of piety.

      c. love can mean many things.

      d. there is only one god, so it cannot be pious to make reference to many.

6. Those Socrates identifies in his speech to the jury as the earlier accusers

      a. are the ones who complained about him to the oracle at Delphi.

      b. he later names as Meletus, Anytus, and Lycon.

      c. have charged him in court with corrupting the youth.

   x d. will be the most difficult to defend himself against.

7. The oracle at Delphi told Socrates' friend that

      a. Socrates was the wisest man alive.

      b. Socrates should spend his life questioning the Athenians about virtue.

   x c. no one was wiser than Socrates.

      d. only the god was wise.

8. One thing Socrates does *not* say during his defense speech at the trial is that

   x a. life is the greatest good.

      b. a good man cannot be harmed.

      c. it is wicked and shameful to do wrong.

      d. it is not difficult to avoid death.

9. The reason Socrates concludes that death is not an evil is that
    a. whatever the many believe is probably wrong.
  x b. his voice did not hinder him in anything he did that day.
    c. it is either a dreamless sleep or conversation with those that died before.
    d. it is not wise to fear something when you do not know whether it is bad.

10. Socrates refuses Crito's offer of escape from prison because
    a. he is already seventy years old and would die soon anyway.
    b. it would be dangerous for his family if he tried to escape.
    c. he doesn't want to be a burden on those who would have to take him in after the escape.
  x d. in escaping he would do injury to the laws of Athens.

B. Short-Answer Questions

Euthyphro

1. Socrates tells Euthyphro that he is searching for the "form" of piety. What does he mean by that?

He wants to know (a) what all examples of piety have in common, (b) what is not shared by any impious actions, and (c) what it is that *makes* something pious.

2. When Euthyphro offers his second try at a definition of piety "what is dear to the gods," Socrates exclaims, "Splendid Euthyphro!" Why?

Because, unlike the first answer, this is at least the right kind of thing. It does try to give the characteristics of the pious and is the sort of thing that could possibly be correct—though it isn't.

3. How does Socrates show Euthyphro that there is something wrong with the definition of piety as "what is dear to the gods" (Euthyphro's second attempt)?

He shows Euthyphro that this definition is inconsistent with other things that Euthyphro himself has asserted—for instance, that there are quarrels among the gods. If the gods disagree, if they don't all love the same things, then—according to this definition—some things will be both pious and impious, since they

27

are loved by some gods and hated by others. But that is impossible, so there is something wrong somewhere.

4. What is Socrates' objection to Euthyphro's claim that what *all* the gods love is what is pious—his third try at an answer?

Socrates says that this only gives him an external quality of the pious—how it is regarded by the gods. But it doesn't tell him what it is to be pious, what *makes* something pious. He believes it is obvious that being loved by the gods is not what makes something pious. But then there must be something about the pious itself that accounts for the fact that they love it. That is what he wants to know—what it is, what its "form" is.

5. Supposing that piety is part of justice, what part of justice is it? And how is that part clarified in the dialog?

It is that part of justice that concerns our relationship to the divine. It is clarified in terms of care of the gods. Not the kind of care a horse trainer has for horses, to be sure, because we cannot benefit the gods or make them better. But the kind of care a servant has for a master.

6. If piety is "a sort of trading skill between gods and men," it seems to follow that what we do for the gods benefits them in some way. How does this consideration lead to a circle in the argument about piety?

It would be *hubris* to think that we mortals could benefit the gods—make them better or happier than they are. So if piety is sacrifice and prayer, giving to the gods and begging from them, it must be valuable to them simply because they like it. So it is what is dear to the gods, what they love. And we are back to the third proposal—that piety is what all the gods love. And we already saw difficulties with that. That is why Socrates declares, "We must investigate again from the beginning what piety is...."

Apology
1. Socrates distinguishes his earlier accusers from the later accusers. Identify each. Which does he consider harder to defend against? Why? And what are their accusations?

The earlier accusers are his fellow citizens who for many years had formed an opinion about him on the basis of rumor and gossip, influenced by some popular and funny plays—for instance, *The Clouds*. This opinion held that he claimed to be a "wise man" who understands "things in the sky and below the earth," who "makes the worse argument into the stronger," and who teaches these

28

things to others. These earlier accusations will be harder to defend against because they are amorphous, anonymous, widespread, and deeply ingrained.

2. How does Socrates try to defend himself against the accusations of the earlier accusers?

Socrates says he has no interest in things in the heavens or under the earth at all and invites those who have heard him to testify whether they have ever heard him discussing these matters. Moreover, he says, he has never been anyone's teacher and calls his poverty to be witness to the fact.

3. What does Socrates do in response to the oracle's claim that there is no one wiser than he? And why?

He is puzzled by the oracle's answer and doesn't understand what the god could mean. He knows he is not what most people consider wise, so he determines to do some field work to try to clarify the meaning. He goes to a series of folks—the politicians, the poets, and the craftsmen—trying to determine whether any of them is wiser than he. He discovers that they all make claims to know things—things that, upon examination, it turns out they don't know at all. So he concludes that he is wiser than they at least in this: that he doesn't claim to know things he really doesn't know.

4. What kind of wisdom does Socrates claim to have? What kind does he lack? Describe each.

He claims to have only "human wisdom," which he says is worth little in comparison to the wisdom of the god. The wisdom of the god would be like that actually had by craftsmen about their craft. It would include an understanding of the "form" of the matter in question, an account of why things are the way they are, an ability to teach these things to others, and the competence to make the knowledge effective in practice. Human knowledge does not understand the form or have an account of why, is not something that can be imparted by teaching, and consists merely in what has not been refuted by the questioning. There is no certainty attached to it. Human wisdom is acutely conscious of its ignorance.

5   Socrates asks Meletus who improves the young if he, Socrates, is their corrupter. What is Meletus' answer? And what is Socrates' critique of this answer?

Meletus at first says the laws improve the young but finally asserts that everyone improves them but Socrates. Socrates responds with a series of analogies, showing in case after case that it is not the many who improve, but only the few. How strange it would be, he says, if in this one case it were just the other way around. No one could believe that.

6. Socrates asks Meletus whether he corrupts the youth intentionally or inadvertently? What sort of bind does this put Meletus in?

If Meletus says "intentionally," Socrates will point out that those who are corrupted harm those about them, and will ask in effect, "How dumb do you think I am? If Meletus says "inadvertently," Socrates will point out that then he needs instruction, not punishment, and should not be on trial but in school.

7. Socrates says, "I have never been anyone's teacher." Why does he feel the need to say this? And what does he mean by it?

Accused of corrupting the youth by teaching them to disregard the city's gods and to reverence other gods, Socrates needs to rebut this charge. It is particularly important to do so because there have been people associated with him whom the jurors have good reason to hate and fear—Critias, the murderous leader of the Thirty; and Alcibiades the traitor. If Socrates is their teacher, he can be held at least partly responsible for their crimes.

He understands his claim to mean that, like a midwife, he can bring to birth only what is already in some sense present within the people he talks to. He imparts nothing. That is why he questions, rather than makes speeches.

8. Why would Socrates refuse an offer to spare his life if only he would cease practicing philosophy?

Because he is convinced that he was set in Athens by "the god" to examine his fellow citizens about *arete*, and to abandon this task just to avoid death would be shameful and cowardly.

9. Why does Socrates, at his trial, refuse to use the traditional "appeal to pity," bringing before the jury his weeping wife and children?

Because it would not be right for him to try to sway them from their duty as jurymen. Their job is to judge on the basis of the evidence presented, and feeling sorry for the defendant is irrelevant to the question of guilt or innocence.

10. What is it that makes Socrates say, after the verdict and the sentencing, that he thinks there is "good hope that death is a blessing"?

The fact that his "voice" did not forbid him at any time during the trial. What he did and said led to the sentence of death. But his voice keeps him from

30

doing things that are harmful. So it must not be that death is an evil, or surely his voice would have prevented his behaving in a way that resulted in his death.

Crito

1. Why does Socrates think one should never do wrong?
Because it is shameful and harmful to the soul of the agent. The most important thing is to care for one's soul, and unjust actions corrupt the most important part of us, making us worse persons. It is not wise to do what makes one worse.

2. What is the reasoning that convinces Socrates that it would be wrong to escape from prison, as Crito urges him to?
To escape would be to break a just agreement he had reached with the laws of Athens by living there so long and contentedly. To break such an agreement is to injure people. To injure people is to do wrong. And one must never do wrong—even if one has been wronged. So it would be wrong for Socrates to escape. So he will not do it.

C. Essay Questions

1. Write a dialogue between Heraclitus (H), Amplicus (A)—a fictional but typical Sophist—and Socrates (S) about whether we can know the truth of things.

2. The Sophists claimed to be wise. Socrates acknowledged that he, too, seemed to possess a certain kind of wisdom. In as many ways as you can, using numbered paragraphs (one for each major point), compare and contrast Socrates' wisdom with that of the Sophists.
(Hints: You might think about *arete*, the measure, weak and strong arguments, true-for-me, the truth, ignorance, winning, teaching, believing in the gods, justice, self-preservation, and so on.)

3. In the *Apology*, Socrates tells the jurors that their killing him will harm them more than it will harm him. He also says that "a good man cannot be harmed either in life or in death." Explain these striking remarks. How do these attitudes play a role in his refusal to escape from prison?

CHAPTER 6
PLATO
Knowing the Real and the Good

ESSENTIAL POINTS

- Knowledge and Opinion
  * The four criteria distinguishing knowledge from opinion
  * How mathematical examples (like doubling the square) show that we do have some knowledge of the truth
  * Why knowledge (which endures) must be about objects that endure
  * The three avenues of approach to the Forms, and how they cohere: epistemological, metaphysical, semantic
- The World and the Forms
  * That Forms both *make intelligible* (*explain*) and *produce* (*bring into being*) things in the visible world
  * The Divided Line
  * Why dialectic leads to ever more fundamental Forms
  * The Form of the Good and the analogy of the sun
  * How skepticism and relativism are refuted (or, at least, why Plato thinks they are)
- Love of Wisdom
  * The Myth of the Cave
  * Correlating the Cave and the Divided Line
  * The ladder of love and its goal: Beauty Itself
- The Soul
  * Why the soul is immortal
  * The three-part structure of the soul; the proper functions of each part
- Justice
  * The argument that justice is good by nature
  * The story of Gyges
  * Happiness as a natural good
  * Happiness as harmony in the soul
  * Internal and external justice
  * The moral of the monster-lion-man image
- The State
  * Philosophers as kings
  * The analogy of the ship

- Problem with the Forms
  * The third-man paradox

TEACHING SUGGESTIONS

1.   Students often think the Forms must be merely ideas or concepts in an individual's mind.
     To counter that tendency, you might point out that when Socrates thought of a square, there was indeed an idea of a square in his mind, but that he wasn't thinking about *that idea:* (a) he used that idea to pick out what he *was* thinking about; (b) it makes no sense to think of ideas as square; and (c) ideas cannot be doubled in size—but squares can.

2.   Students find it hard to take seriously the thought that things in the visible world are not the most real of things.
     To give Plato a run for his money, emphasize that this is a mere prejudice on their part, and that we have to go where the best argument leads.

3.   Students may find it hard to grasp that the Divided Line and the Myth of the Cave tell basically the same story.
     Show them the parallels in detail. The new cave drawing in the third edition may help.

4.   Students often find obscure the idea of dialectic in the higher reaches of the Divided Line.
     I use the argument about justice as an example to show how dialectical reasoning can demonstrate that one Form (Justice) participates in another (the Good).

EXAM QUESTIONS
A. Multiple-Choice Questions

1.   Knowing something, according to Plato,
        a. requires having evidence provided by your senses.
     x b. puts you in touch with reality.
        c. is the result of persuasion.
        d. means it is very unlikely that you are mistaken about it, though that is always possible.

33

2. The objects of knowledge, Plato says, are
   a. things you can see and touch.
   b. the things believed in by everyone in your culture.
   c. items in flux, continually changing from moment to moment.
   x d. Forms (intelligible realities).

3. Forms are related to visible things by being
   a. mirror images of them.
   b. ideas of them in our minds.
   x c. their cause and explanation.
   d. identical with the class of things having something in common with a given thing.

4. In Plato's Divided Line,
   a. the sections must be equal in length to do the symbolic job he requires of them.
   x b. the intelligible world is related to the visible world as visible things are related to images of them.
   c. the intelligible world is related to the visible world as images are related to the things of which they are images.
   d. science is portrayed as the way to ultimate truth, where the soul can "rest from the road."

5. The Form of the Good
   a. is explained by Plato in terms of still other Forms.
   b. is the one and only Form that can be seen with the naked eye.
   x c. is the ultimate explainer.
   d. is located by Plato in the absolute center of the Divided Line.

6. Plato tells us the Form of the Good is like the sun in
   a. dazzling our eyes when we first look at it.
   b. being located at the extreme end of the intelligible world on the Divided Line.
   c. no way whatsoever.
   x d. being to truth and knowledge what the sun is to light and sight.

7. In the Myth of the Cave,
    x a. the prisoners represent all of us before we begin to search for wisdom.
    b. the prisoners are forced to look directly at the fire, though that hurts their eyes.
    c. the exit represents access to the visible world, lighted by the sun.
    d. no one who escapes and sees reality as it is would ever return to that dismal place.

8. According to Plato, education is
    a. supplying the facts to those who need them.
    b. everyone's job.
    c. valuable because it pays off in the acquisition of marketable skills.
    x d. turning the soul of the student toward the real.

9. The ladder of love
    a. begins with a vision of Beauty itself, and leads beyond it.
    x b. leads its climbers to more and more satisfying objects of love.
    c. begins with erotic love (*eros*), but leads the climber beyond it to an altogether different kind of love.
    d. shows us a pattern that is precisely the reverse of that we find on the Divided Line.

10. Philosophy, Plato says, is "training for dying." He says this because
    x a. philosophizing attaches us to intelligible realities, separating us from the body.
    b. he realizes we all fear death and need help to approach it with courage.
    c. philosophers hate life.
    d. the wise Silenus has said that the best thing for a human being is not to be, and the next best thing is to die soon.

11. The soul, Plato tells us, has distinct parts, each of which has a function. For instance:
    a. the ego, which is the reality principle.
    b. the id, or the set of unconscious desires present in every soul.
    c. the superego, or conscience.
  x d. reason, which guides.

12. Happiness, according to Plato, is
    a. a matter of how you feel.
    b. determined by how many of your desires are satisfied.
  x c. a condition of harmony among the parts of the soul.
    d. something even a bad person can experience.

13. A just person
    a. may have a rough time in life but will be admired by all in the end.
    b. may or may not be a happy person.
    c. is the person considered by a community to be just.
  x d. will be a happy person.

14. The lesson of the sailors-on-the-ship analogy is that
  x a. statesmanship, like navigation, requires knowledge.
    b. sailors are generally an unruly lot.
    c. whoever has power in a state had better watch out, for there are always others ready to snatch it away.
    d. democracy is the best form of government.

15. The paradox of the third man
    a. is resolved by Plato, who shows decisively that it poses no danger to his views.
  x b. arises from principles to which Plato is deeply committed.
    c. proves that Plato's doctrine of the Forms is correct.
    d. involves at least three male human beings.

B. Short-Answer Questions

1. Draw Plato's Divided Line in the correct proportions, label each section, and explain what the proportionality symbolizes.

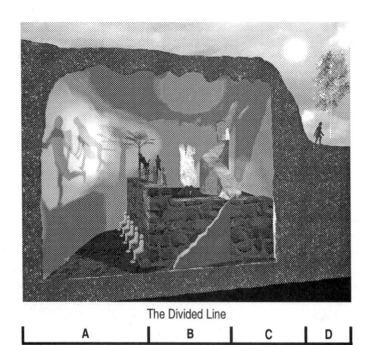

The Divided Line

| A | B | C | D |

A is to B as C is to D, and also as A + B is to C + D.

We are to learn from the line that visible things are related to intelligible Forms in just the way shadows are related to the visible things that cast them. Visible things are brought into being by the Forms (just as a tree shadow is produced by the tree). And they are made intelligible by the Forms (just as we understand the shape of a shadow when we are acquainted with the thing whose shadow it is).

2. Distinguish knowledge from opinion.

Knowledge is always true, endures, is backed up by reasons (a *logos*), and is the result of instruction. Opinion may be true or false, may or may not last, is not backed up soundly by reasons, and is produced in us by persuasion.

3. What does an educator do for those he or she "teaches"?

An educator "turns" the soul of the student away from shadows and mere opinion toward reality. When our gaze is directed toward the real, we grasp the truth for ourselves. That is why one person never really "teaches" another anything. The most a "teacher" can do is point a student in the right direction.

4. What are the parts of the soul? What are their functions?

There are three. *Desire*, or appetite, motivates us to action. *Spirit* (emotion) gives life its sparkle, zest, and makes living enjoyable. And our *reason*, seeking wisdom, guides the soul. A healthy, happy soul is one in which each of the three parts is doing its thing with excellence, neither thwarting nor trying to take over the proper functions of the other parts.

5. How is "internal justice" related to "social justice"? Explain this in terms of the role of *the monster* in Plato's image of the man composed of a lion, a man, and a monster.

An internally just person is one in whom the parts of the soul do not "overreach" themselves and take over the functions of other parts. If the monster represents the desires we experience (some wild and fierce, some tame and useful), then one way of having an unjust soul would be to let desire dictate how we live—disregarding the admonitions of reason and overriding them to pursue what we so much *want*. The external result of such a disordered soul will necessarily be a person who is unjust to other persons—trying in every way to get the advantage over them, without any hindrance from reason and the Good. In contrast, a person whose soul is in harmony will not be unjust to others, because desire will be controlled by reason.

6. Who should rule in a good state, according to Plato? And why?

Philosophers should rule, because they and only they know what is best, what a good state is and how a good person should live. Philosophers understand the meaning of Justice and of the Good. Plato said we could not have a good state until either kings become philosophers or philosophers become kings.

7. Using an example, sketch the "third-man paradox," the problem Plato himself recognizes with the theory of the Forms.

Two objects are both large, say a hippo and an elephant. They therefore share the Form of the Large. But, according to Plato, a Form itself has the characteristics it explains in particular things; in other words, the Form of the Large is itself large. But now we have *three* large things, the hippo, the elephant, and the Form. These three things have something in common, largeness, and this requires explanation.

Plato's explanation is that they share a Form, so there must be a second, and then a third and a fourth Form, to explain the commonalities in things that are large. *And so on!* Here is an infinite regress that Plato himself cannot stop from occurring in his theory of Forms.

8. If Plato's Socrates has it right, through what stages must a lover move if he/she is to find ultimate satisfaction?

Loving first a beautiful body, then all beautiful bodies. Then the souls that animate those bodies. Then the laws and institutions that produce beautiful souls. Then the knowledge that makes possible those laws and institutions. And finally, in an ecstatic vision, Beauty itself, that which produces and makes intelligible all beautiful things.

9.   What do you think Antiphon, or Callicles, or Thrasymachus (or some other imagined Sophist) might say in response to Plato's argument that justice is intrinsically good—good as a matter of *physis*?

Nice job Plato! Quite a good *logos* you constructed there. But I can give you one equally good. What makes any living thing happy? Getting what it desires. So don't give me this stuff about "harmony in the soul." Social justice, expressed in the laws of *nomos*, is just a tactic created by the strong and powerful in a society to maximize their desire satisfactions. So why should the rest of us help them out? It's dog eat dog in this world, everyone for himself. That's the reality. And if something seems just to me (or to Athens), who are you to tell me (or Athens) otherwise? Your opinion is no better than mine. So stick it in your ear, Plato, and leave me alone to feed my "beast."

10. Use Plato's analogy of the ship, the sailors, and the navigator to explain why he thinks democracy is a poor form of government.

All the sailors on the ship think they can navigate as well as anyone, and they plot to seize control of the ship, to overthrow the owner, and run things as they see best. But none of them has studied navigation. So how can they bring the ship safely to port, or sail it securely on the open sea? A good navigator has *knowledge*. And so must a good *statesman*. Those who would guide the "ship of state" must know what justice is and wherein lies the Good for the city. Just as not everyone is a competent navigator, not everyone can be supposed to possess the craft of statesmanship. That is reserved for the few—those who have been educated in the Forms.

11. How does Plato use mathematics/geometry to refute the skepticism and relativism of the Sophists?

Plato claims that there are things we know—for instance, that the diagonal of a square can be used to create a square twice the area of the original. Therefore knowledge is not unobtainable, and the skeptics are mistaken. Also this knowledge is unchangeable and true for everyone, everywhere. So the relativists are mistaken.

12. If the slave boy had never been instructed in geometry and yet can recognize the correct answer to a geometrical problem, what

conclusion does Plato's Socrates think we should draw?

That everyone has a previous knowledge of the Forms. We all know these truths before birth, but once we are born into a body, our knowledge is erased. Our lives are quests to regain the knowledge we lost at birth. We learn these things not through being told them by someone claiming to "know," but by being pointed in the right direction, just as Socrates did for the slave boy. When we pay attention in the right way, we "recollect" the truth that we once knew explicitly.

13. What does Plato think Justice consists of—in the individual soul and in the state?

The parts of a soul, just as the citizens of a state, have characteristic functions. In the soul, desire motivates, spirit animates, and reason rules. In the state, some produce goods, some defend against enemies, and some govern. In both, Justice amounts to each part performing its function without overreaching itself and encroaching on the proper function of the other parts.

14. For Plato, how is the Form of the Good like the Sun?

Plato tells us that he cannot *explain* the Good, but he can tell us what it is like: It is like the sun. In what ways? Well, the sun produces and makes possible all the visible realities in our world—without the sun, no earth, warmth, life. And it explains or makes intelligible the fact that all these many things exist in our world. In the same way, the Form of the Good makes intelligible and produces everything else, both in the visible world and the intelligible.

15. Why does Plato think that mathematical knowledge cannot be *about* the things of this visible world?

Because it is perfectly exact, and nothing in this world is so perfect. And because it is unchanging, which is true of nothing in visible reality.

16. Sketch the *epistemological* argument for the Forms.

We do have knowledge, and such knowledge is enduring. Nothing in the visible world endures, so our knowledge must be about other realities—the Forms. Moreover, what we know can be perfectly precise—e.g., that the sum of the interior angles of a triangle equals two right angles. But we can't draw or construct a triangle like that—and if we had one before us we couldn't verify that it was one. So the object of our knowledge must be other than what we can see and touch—again, the Forms.

17. Sketch the *metaphysical* argument for the Forms.

Two things in the visible world may share some characteristic; for instance, they may both be square. So they have something in common. But what they have in common cannot be identical with either one; nor is it identical with the two things taken together. So what they have in common must be distinct from either one. It is, in fact, Plato concludes, the Form of the Square, in which each participates.

C. Essay Questions

1.   How does Plato understand Education? Relate education to the distinction between opinion and knowledge, to his analysis of love, to the divided line, and to the cave.

2.   What is Plato's argument that Justice is a natural good? Relate it to the myth of Gyges; to the myth of the charioteer; and to the image of the man, the lion, and the monster.

3.   Draw and explain Plato's Divided Line. Show how it fits with the Myth of the Cave, the Analogy of the Sun, and with Plato's view of Education.

4.   Discuss Plato's theory of the Forms and how they relate to the visible things of this world. Show how themes from both Heraclitus and Parmenides are woven into this theory.

5.   Tell the "Ring of Gyges" story. Then sketch Plato's view of the soul, by which Plato means to convince us that the shepherd would have been *happier* if he had resisted the temptations of the ring—if he had acted justly rather than unjustly.

6.   You (yes, *you*) are Plato. You hear someone expressing the following views:
    "Don't give me this crap about 'justice.' We all know that 'justice' is a matter of the law. And who makes the law? Those in power make the law. And for whose benefit do they make it? For their own, of course. You are so naive! For most of us, being 'just' is a *disadvantage,* not a good thing— except as a sort of strategy for managing in society without getting clobbered. Something good in itself? Don't make me laugh."
What do you say?

41

CHAPTER 7
ARISTOTLE
The Reality of the World

ESSENTIAL POINTS

Note: I do not spend much class time on the contrasts drawn early in the chapter between Aristotle and Plato, but refer back to them as they come up in the details of the chapter.

- Logic and Knowledge
  * That logic supplies a nonpsychological criterion for goodness in argument (compare to the Sophists)
  * Statements are sentences that can be true or false; the functions of subject and predicate
  * Terms make up statements
  * Kinds of terms—the categories; the fundamental character of terms for primary substances
  * Truth as correspondence
  * The formal character of logic
  * The Square of Opposition and the Syllogism
  * Induction as the means to know universal first principles and stop an infinite regress
- The World
  * The distinction between artifacts and nature-facts; the distinguishing character of nature-facts
  * The four causes: material, formal, efficient, and final
  * The character of teleology; its connection with potentiality and the lawfulness of change
  * That the natural world is knowable, so there is no reason to demote it to second-class reality status
- First Philosophy
  * Four reasons why Aristotle does not accept Plato's account of the Forms
  * How mathematics is possible without Plato's Forms: abstraction
  * Why form is prior even to substance
  * What kind of form an essence is
  * The possibility of pure forms, pure actualities
  * God as final cause of the world; the unmoved mover

* The possibility of pure forms, pure actualities
* God as final cause of the world; the unmoved mover
- The Soul
  * That the three levels of soul build on each other
  * That soul is fundamentally nonsubstantial, but is the form of a living body of a certain sort
  * Why Aristotle cannot find a material substratum for the activities of *nous,* and concludes that it must have an independent and immortal existence
- The Good Life
  * Why precise answers are not available for questions about the best life or the right thing to do in a given circumstance
  * Why happiness—*eudaemonia*—is not pleasure or honor
  * Why happiness is *activity,* why it is activity of *soul,* why it is in accord with *reason,* and why it is *excellence* in the performance of that activity
  * Why, and how, the good life includes pleasure
  * That a happy life requires modest external goods
  * What kind of thing a virtue is: a habit or disposition
  * That the virtues are attained by practice
  * That virtue lies in a mean between extremes
  * That the function of reason is to discover the mean for us in a given circumstance
  * How Aristotle's ethics is not Sophistic relativism but involves a kind of objective relativity
  * That Aristotle assumes we are responsible for our actions unless we can provide an excuse
  * That legitimate excuses are of two sorts: ignorance (of facts) and compulsion
  * That the very best life is a life of contemplation—a life most like the life of God

TEACHING SUGGESTIONS

1.   Develop examples of syllogisms different from those in the text. You want some that
   - have true premises and are valid (demonstrations).
   - are valid but do not have true premises.
   - have true premises but are invalid.

2. I require students to memorize Aristotle's definition of truth. It is short, elegant, and important.

3. Euclid's axioms are a good example of what Aristotle has in mind when he talks of first principles—familiar because the students have all studied geometry.

4. In discussing Aristotle on nature-facts, I find it useful to bring a prop—an orange, perhaps, or an apple or banana (whatever I'm having for lunch that day!). The four causes can be nicely illustrated with such an example, too.

5. It is *very* hard to get students to grasp Aristotle's fundamental view of soul. They invariably think in terms of a thing or substance. Use examples like the eye or the axe or the wax seal, and keep hammering away at the idea of *function*.

6. When discussing Aristotle's critique of pleasure as the good, I tell students a little story. I have, I say, a machine. If they will get into it, this machine will give them—guaranteed—a life of more pleasure than they could get any other way. (You can elaborate on this in any number of directions.) Then I ask them how many would like to get into my machine—Oh, wait, I say, there's one thing I forgot to tell them. Once you get into the machine, you can never get out again. But—incredible pleasures for the rest of your life! Then I ask them how many want to get in. Interesting results.

7. Students have a tendency to conclude that for Aristotle the good life is the life of contemplation—maybe because that is discussed last. Emphasize that there are many kinds of good lives exemplifying many kinds of virtues. True, there is one that is *best*. But it is not Aristotle's view that only the philosopher can live a good human life.

8. At some point you may want to make use of the symbolism in Raphael's painting on the cover, with Plato pointing upward and Aristotle having his hand out flat—each indicating what he takes to be reality.

EXAM QUESTIONS
A. Multiple-Choice Questions

1. A statement, according to Aristotle, is
    - a. like a prayer.
    - b. composed of three or more terms.
    - c. like knowledge, always true.
    - x d. either true or false.

2. In a syllogism,
    - a. the conclusion follows from the premises.
    - x b. there are always exactly three terms.
    - c. the premises must be true if the conclusion is true.
    - d. if the premises are true, the conclusion must be true.

3. The first principles of a science are
    - x a. the clearest and most certain things we know.
    - b. arrived at by demonstration.
    - c. proved to be true through syllogistic reasoning.
    - d. unknowable.

4. In Aristotle's account of the four causes,
    - a. the efficient cause of the world is God.
    - b. a final cause is pure potentiality.
    - c. the formal cause is the shape that a material object has in three dimensions.
    - x d. the material cause is the one that explains the individuality of things.

5. Pleasure, for Aristotle, is
    - a. never to be sought as an end.
    - b. the end by which humans are naturally motivated.
    - x c. unsuitable as the principal end for rational creatures.
    - d. the reason we should be virtuous.

6. Virtue, Aristotle says, is defined by a mean relative to us. He means that

    x a. facts about an individual and her circumstances are relevant to what should be done.
       b. we all have different values.
       c. if you think *x* is the right thing to do, who's to say you are wrong?
       d. there are no virtues common to all.

7. Suppose I do something wrong but offer an excuse. Which of these excuses, if true, would be acceptable, according to Aristotle?

       a. I didn't know it was wrong.
       b. My parents mistreated me when I was young.
       c. I did it to Jones because Jones did it to me.
    x d. I was forced to do it.

8. God, Aristotle says,

       a. cares for his creatures as a father cares for his child.
    x b. functions as the final cause for the world.
       c. knows the number of hairs on each person's head.
       d. is a moved unmover.

9. Soul, according to Aristotle, is

       a. the unique possession of rational creatures such as humans.
       b. a primary substance.
       c. common to all nature-facts.
    x d. the form of a living body.

10. Aristotle defines happiness (*eudaemonia*) as

       a. harmony in the soul.
       b. a feeling of excellence (*arete*) pervading the soul.
    x c. activity of the soul in accord with reason.
       d. whatever makes you feel good about yourself.

11. Aristotle differs from Plato in
    a. believing knowledge is different from opinion.
  x b. holding that something like a puppy is as real as anything can be.
    c. loving wisdom less.
    d. being more otherworldly than Plato.

12. Aristotle explains change in terms of
    a. atoms and the void.
    b. flux and opposition.
    c. the vortex motion of the universe.
  x d. actuality and potentiality.

13. Nature is purposive, Aristotle says, in virtue of
    a. the plan God had in mind when he created nature.
    b. intentions resident in every nature-fact.
  x c. the entelechy resident in things.
    d. our using nature for our own purposes.

B. Short-Answer Questions

1. What distinguishes *primary substance* from all the other categories?

    (a) Terms for primary substances can fill only one place in statement—that of the subject. They cannot be predicates of other things. ("This apple is red," but not "Red is this apple.") Terms belonging to other categories can fill either place. ("This apple is red," and "Red is my favorite color.") (b) Primary substance is basic; it alone can exist independently. It is that to which features such as quality, quantity, and position belong.

2. What is truth?

    To say of what is that it is, and of what is not that it is not, is true. So truth is a property of certain statements, relating them to what they are about.

3. Does Aristotle's logic do anything to resolve the problems posed by the Sophists' teaching of rhetoric?

    It provides a criterion for evaluating the goodness of an argument (validity), which is independent of the persuasiveness of the argument. Validity is solely a matter of *form* and is intrinsic to the argument, whereas persuasiveness is an external matter of how the argument affects people. Thus it allows for the detection of bad arguments, which nonetheless happen to persuade.

4. What is a *first principle*? Why are first principles needed? How are they known?

A first principle is a definition for a class of things (a species). It gives the essence—tells us *what* a thing is. First principles are needed because reasons cannot be given (in syllogistic form) for every truth—otherwise we would be involved in an infinite regress. They are known through *induction*, that process leading from experience through memory to the correct classification of things by *nous,* the active principle of knowing in the soul.

5. What is an *essence*?

An essence is a form belonging to a substance; it is the form that makes the substance the thing that it is. Without the characteristics comprising the essence, the thing could not be what it is.

6. What is God like? What kind of cause is God?

God is a pure substance, one containing no matter. God is wholly actual, without any potentiality at all, and hence eternal, active, and alive. God thinks only the best thoughts, about the best thing, himself, and God is the final cause of the world—i.e., what everything else imitates to the extent possible for it, the goal for all the world's striving.

7. Characterize the three kinds of soul?

(a) Nutritive soul: that possessed by plants, making possible nutrition and reproduction

(b) Sensitive soul: that possessed by animals, comprising sensation and movement

(c) Rational soul: that possessed by humans, making language and reasoning possible

8. How is soul related to body?

A soul is the form of a body of a certain kind (plant, animal, or human) that potentially has life. A soul actualizes that potentiality. So a soul is not a part of a body; nor is it an independent substance. It is to the body as sight is to the eyes. (What Aristotle says about *nous,* however, is inconsistent with this main answer.)

9. How does pleasure come into the good life?

Pleasure cannot come into the good life as its goal. To take pleasure as our goal would be to diminish ourselves, striving for what is proper to the non-rational animals. Yet the good life is a pleasant one—because we do find the most excellent exercise of our capacities to be pleasurable—and the good life is excellent (virtuous) activity of soul in accord with reason. So the good life is also the happy life. But to seek for pleasure as our end is to miss the most excellent of activities.

10. Explain Aristotle's doctrine of the *mean*.

The mean lies between extremes of excess and deficiency, along the line of some feeling or action open to us—e.g., fear, anger, or sharing our goods. The mean that is excellent is not necessarily the mathematical mean (or average) but is relative to the situation; so the wise person is angry to a certain degree for certain reasons depending on the time, the occasion, and the persons involved.

11. What is *practical wisdom*?

Practical wisdom is the capacity to find the mean in a particular situation. It is different from theoretical wisdom (which is the understanding of the natures of things and their reasons-why) in that it is directed to *particular* situations: How does a brave person act in *these* circumstances? It is our rational capacity in the service of action, determining what would be the excellent or virtuous thing to do.

12. Does having a bad character excuse a person? Explain.

No. Aristotle holds that our character is a result of the actions we have taken in the past. So we are not the victims of our character (as though we were *compelled* by it), but its creators. Since we have made ourselves what we are by our past actions, there is no excuse if now we act badly because we have a bad character. We should have known that we were creating a bad person. Moreover, we can change our character in the same way it was formed—by practice.

13. What is a *syllogism*? Give an example (different from any in the text). What are the two good-making features of arguments, according to Aristotle? Does your example satisfy those criteria?

A syllogism is an argument composed of three subject-predicate judgments, each containing just two terms. The two premises contain a term in common, known as the middle term, whose function is to provide a link between the subject and predicate terms that occur in the conclusion.

All terrorists are pussy cats.
No pussy cats are fierce.
So, no terrorists are fierce.

To be sound (good) an argument must (a) have true premises and (b) be valid. This syllogism is not a good argument, though valid, because it does not have true premises.

14. How does Aristotle's *unmoved mover* move things other than itself?

By attraction. Being pure form, unmixed with matter, the unmoved mover is also pure actuality. It is what everything would be if it could, or that to which things attempt to approximate insofar as it is possible for them. Being that toward which everything strives, it puts them into motion in the way a final cause does.

C. Essay Questions

1. (a) Explain the development of an acorn into an oak tree in an Aristotelian manner, using the concepts of *matter* and *form, potentiality* and *actuality,* together with the *four causes.* (b) Contrast this with an atomist account of the same phenomena.

2. Explain Aristotle's doctrine of virtue, bringing in the concepts of a mean, practical wisdom, and the relation of virtue to happiness.

3. Compare Aristotle's view of knowledge with that of Plato. What are its characteristics? What are its objects? By what procedures can we come to know?

4. Compare Aristotle and Plato on the question of reality. What kinds of things are most real? Why?

5. Compare Aristotle and Plato on the nature of the soul, including its relationship to the body. Do not neglect to bring Aristotle's concept of *nous* into the picture.

CHAPTER 8
EPICUREANS, STOICS, AND SKEPTICS
Happiness for the Many

ESSENTIAL POINTS

- Epicureans
  * Happiness consists in pleasure: hedonism
  * Philosophy as a guide for maximizing the pleasant life
  * Atomism dispels certain fears
    — About the gods
    — About death
  * The smart hedonist does not pursue every pleasure
  * Wisdom distinguishes among desires
    — Natural/vain
    — Merely natural/necessary
    — Necessary for happiness/for ease/for life
  * The simple life as the good and happy life
  * The importance of friendship
- Stoics
  * The crucial distinction: between what is in our power and what is not in our power
  * Our happiness and our freedom is completely in our power—in how we deal with events that happen
  * Keeping our wills in harmony with nature
  * Reality as material, ordered by a *logos*, and so also divine
  * The naturalness of what is preferred, what is shunned, and what is indifferent to us
  * The only true good is virtue
  * Pleasure is *never* to be taken as an end
  * Intentions as the mark of goodness in a person
  * Duty and the universality of law
- Skeptics
  * Modes of skeptical reasoning
    — From the differences among sense organs
    — From differences among human beings
    — Infinite regress and circular reasoning problems
  * The problem of the criterion
  * Living according to appearances
  * Happiness as tranquility of soul

TEACHING SUGGESTIONS

1. After struggling through Plato and Aristotle, students usually find these thinkers quite accessible—and attractive. I have sometimes taken advantage of this by staging a debate among those favoring one or another view of the good life. Students are allowed to choose whether to defend a Platonist, an Aristotelian, an Epicurean, a Stoic, or a Skeptical approach to the issue. Then these five groups meet independently for twenty minutes or so, planning their defense—and also criticisms of rival views. The rest of the class period is spent in discussion. It can be very lively.

2. Students sometimes say that Epicurus thinks *too much* pleasure is a bad thing. You can point out that since pleasure is the Good, that is not a possibility for him. You *cannot* have too much pleasure. It is only a question of maximizing this good thing in the long run—and Epicurus is convinced that moderation is the right *means* for doing that.

EXAM QUESTIONS
A. Multiple-Choice Questions

1. Epicurus thinks an important key to happiness lies in natural science because
    - a. it leads to technological breakthroughs that enhance the quality of life.
    - x b. it can show us that some of our fears are unfounded.
    - c. knowledge is something good in itself.
    - d. we should aim to keep our wills in harmony with nature.

2. Hedonism
    - a. recommends pursuing every pleasure, so as to maximize happiness in life.
    - b. is a doctrine that disparages pleasure and recommends virtue as the key to happiness.
    - x c. is compatible with denying oneself many pleasures.
    - d. has nothing to say about pain, fear, or sorrow.

3. We do not need to fear the gods, Epicurus says, because
   x a. they are uninterested in us.
   b. gods are by nature loving and kind.
   c. there are no gods.
   d. when we are, death is not; and when death is, we are not.

4. According to Epicurus, someone who thinks happiness is pleasure and the absence of pain will
   a. be unjust to others, if it will increase pleasure for oneself.
   b. indulge her every desire.
   c. be an untrustworthy friend.
   x d. be content with having little.

5. A Stoic
   x a. believes that our happiness or unhappiness is *entirely* within our own control.
   b. says "Grin and bear it," no matter how unhappy something makes her.
   c. cares for no one and nothing but his own freedom and happiness.
   d. prefers nothing, shuns nothing, and is indifferent to everything.

6. When Stoics advise us to keep our wills in harmony with nature, they
   a. mean that if something feels natural to us, we should "go with the flow."
   b. deny God.
   c. contradict Plato and Aristotle, who emphasize living in accord with reason.
   x d. are in effect advising us to do our duty.

7. A Stoic thinks we should
   a. seek virtue more than happiness.
   x b. never seek pleasure as an end.
   c. always be virtuous, because virtue produces the greatest pleasure.
   d. be skeptical of all claims to know what virtue is.

8. A Skeptic will
    a. assert that nothing can be known.
    b. assert that we can know only the contents of our own minds.
x   c. suspend judgment about what reality is like.
    d. refuse to ask why.

9. With respect to the question, "Does a criterion of truth exist?" the Skeptic
    a. asserts with Xenophanes of Colophon that it does not.
    b. claims that an infinite regress is the only criterion available.
    c. engages in circular reasoning to prove the existence of a criterion.
x   d. suspends judgment.

10. Happiness, says the Skeptic,
    a. is unavailable to humans, because knowledge is unavailable.
    b. must be founded on sure and certain understanding of the true nature of reality.
    c. is available only to those who have gone through the pangs of skeptical doubt and come out into the clear light of knowledge on the other side.
x   d. is a byproduct of giving up the demand to know.

B. Short-Answer Questions

1. For what kinds of pains does Epicurus believe there is a remedy? And what is it?

There are pains we suffer because of beliefs we have—particularly fear of death and fear of the gods, which depend on certain beliefs about death and gods. Those fears can be removed by correct beliefs, which are a result of correct philosophy—which he believes the atomists provide. So we need not fear death because there will be no sensations after death, and so no pains; when we are, death is not; and when death is, we are not. And we need not fear the gods because they have no concern with us and our lives; they do not interfere to cause us pain.

2. What one objection does Epicurus have to the atomism of Democritus? And how does he propose to improve atomism to meet that objection?

Epicurus objects to the mechanical necessity that holds sway over the Democritean universe. If everything happens with necessity, how can we have any choice, any control over our destiny? How can we determine to live more wisely in the pursuit of pleasure, and so become more happy? He imports a "swerve" to the atoms. Sometimes they *unaccountably* swerve. And in those swerves is the foundation for our free will.

3. Given that Epicureans think pleasure is the sole good, why do they praise moderation?

Pleasure is the result of our desires being satisfied. But trying to satisfy each and every desire is unwise, as it will lead to more pain and frustration than necessary. There are vain desires, such as being popular, or having what everyone else has (or more); indulging such desires will never leave one satisfied. And there are desires that are natural but unnecessary to satisfy; those are likely to be more trouble than they are worth. So one should be moderate and try to satisfy only the necessary desires, because what you want is *the most pleasure possible over a complete lifetime.*

4. Epictetus, the Stoic, says that we can be assured of happiness and freedom if we remember always to make one crucial distinction. What is it? And how does making it provide such benefits?

We should always distinguish what is in our power (within our control) from what is not in our power (beyond our control). What is in our power is our beliefs about things, our desires and aversions—how we take things. What is not in our power is everything else, including our body, our reputation, other people, and so on. If we restrict ourselves to what is in our power, no one can ever harm us— since what we *count* as harm is up to us. And nothing can every hinder or constrain or compel us—as it is always up to us how to take such things. So we can always be happy and free.

5. Barbra Streisand sings, "People who need people are the luckiest people in the world." You are a Stoic philosopher. Talk to her.

Barbra, Barbra, you will never be happy living like that. Don't you realize that *needing* people is making yourself dependent on what is not in your own control. How foolish! You put your happiness in the hands of someone else, like a hostage. You say, "Here, do with it what you want; I give you the power to make me unhappy." And you do this yourself! When will you realize that no one else can make you unhappy or put you in bondage? When will you realize that if you restrict yourself to what is *your own,* you will really be, as that song about "Woman" claims, "invincible"? But not with this "needing" stuff. No, no. Give it up, Barbra. Get wise.

6. Explain the skeptical "problem of the criterion."

Suppose we claim to know something; call it *P.* We can be asked about the criterion or standard by which we decide that *P* is something we know. Either *that* is something we claim to know or it is not. If it is not claimed as known, the proper response is to suspend judgment. If we do claim to know it, we can be asked by what criterion we know it. And the question repeats itself. This iteration will either go in a circle and come back to something earlier (in which case we should suspend judgment) or it will go on forever in an infinite regress (in which case we should suspend judgment). In any case, the correct response is to suspend judgment, to make no claims to know what is true.

7. What does it mean when the Skeptic recommends that we "suspend judgment"? About what? Why? And will that be good for us?

To suspend judgment is to refrain from assenting or dissenting, from committing oneself to yes or no about any belief concerning reality—what is really true. The Skeptic thinks that as long as we care about having true beliefs, about *getting it right,* we will be disturbed and liable to be upset by contrary opinions. But if we can come to the point of suspending judgment about these matters, we can live according to appearances—including the customs of our culture—and be happy. So it will be good for us, for we all want to be happy.

C. Essay Questions

1. How do Stoics and Epicureans differ with respect to the role of pleasure in the happy life?

2. Of the Epicureans, the Stoics, and the Skeptics, which are most like the Sophists? Why? And how are they unlike?

3. Do Plato and Aristotle have an answer to the problem of the criterion? If so, what is it? If not, why not?

CHAPTER 9
THE CHRISTIANS
Sin, Salvation, and Love

ESSENTIAL POINTS

- Background
  * There is one God, creator of the universe.
  * The world is created good.
  * Humans fall away from obedience and into sin.
  * Attempts to restore the "kingdom" of God: Noah, Abraham, the Exodus, the giving of the Law, the proclamations of the prophets.
  * The hope for a "Messiah."
- Jesus
  * Proclaims that the "kingdom" is at hand.
  * Indifferent to wealth and social position.
  * Demands absolute love for God and loving one's neighbor as oneself.
  * Internalizes and deepens the Law.
  * Put to death; said to have risen again.
- The Meaning of Jesus
  * Said to be the incarnation of the *logos,* according to which the world was created, the clearest manifestation on earth of the nature of God.
  * In his death and resurrection, said to have redeemed humanity, bearing our guilt in our place.
  * Freed from the need to justify ourselves, we are free in gratitude to live in love as we have been loved.

TEACHING SUGGESTIONS

This short chapter, though not strictly philosophical, serves as a brief introduction to Christian thought, which (a) has been a great influence on the conversation and (b) is virtually unknown by many students today—though many have vague and mistaken impressions of it. It should be approached as a useful prolegomenon to understanding Augustine. Be sure that the main outlines of the problem Augustine addresses are made clear: There is something so drastically wrong in human life that humans cannot straighten it out, and that God in Christ has done that for us.

EXAM QUESTIONS
A. Multiple-Choice Questions

1. According to Jewish and Christian tradition,
    a. the world is just a shadowy image of true reality.
    b. humans were from the very first sinful and disobedient.
    c. the Kingdom of God has little to do with life in this world but is something we can hope to attain in the afterlife.
    x d. God established a covenant with Abraham.

2. Jesus says,
    a. "Take care for your soul, which is your pure and noble essence, that it remain undefiled."
    b. "How hard it will be for those who are poor to enter into the Kingdom of God."
    x c. "As you wish that men would do to you, do so to them."
    d. "No one can serve two masters; indeed, serve no master at all if you would be free."

3. Jesus says,
    x a. "There will be more joy in heaven over one sinner who repents than over ninety-nine righteous persons who need no repentance."
    b. "An eye for an eye and a tooth for a tooth."
    c. "Resist those who are evil; be not contaminated by association with sinners."
    d. "Be not angry with your brother, unless he brings you into judgment."

4. Christians believe that
   a. humans can be justified only by observing all the precepts of the Law.
   x b. the very wisdom through which the world was made can be found in the life and character of Jesus.
   c. our salvation will be accomplished through knowledge and education.
   d. the Jewish Old Testament must be repudiated by believers in Jesus.

5. St. Paul taught that
   a. the soul is essentially good, and salvation consists of becoming aware of who you are.
   b. Jesus and Socrates are much alike—men of virtue whom it would be wise to imitate.
   x c. the will is in conflict with itself and we cannot save ourselves.
   d. unless we live good lives, we cannot inherit the Kingdom of Heaven.

B. Short-Answer Questions

1. What is the "kingdom of God," according to the Christians? And what sort of *love*, according to Jesus, is its heart and center?

   The kingdom of God is a community of righteousness, united in justice under the rule of the creator of the universe. It is present wherever the love of God governs the hearts of human beings, and it will find its consummation with all the saints in a blessed life after death. The love in question is the sort of love demonstrated to us in the life and death of Jesus of Nazareth: giving, forgiving, compassionate, sacrificial. The good Samaritan story is a symbolic representation of what it is like.

2. "In the beginning was the word . . . and the word was made flesh and dwelt among us." What does this mean?

   The "word" in question is the *logos*, the wisdom of God according to which the created world was made. It is this divine *logos* that governs and explains the world. This very *logos*, John tells us, is also present in this one man, Jesus. So Jesus shows us the very nature of reality—the reality of God and also of the world we live in. Reality is governed by love.

3. What is wrong with humans, and how can that be corrected?

The fundamental problem in human life is sin, which is disobedience and rebellion against the creator. Humans want to make their own rules, to seek their own good their own way. So they stray from their nature (which was created good), find themselves divided against themselves, and do not have the health or strength to find their way back to the good life. God, in love, forgives the sinfulness and re-adopts the wayward human into his family. All that is needed is for the human to accept this.

C. Essay Questions

1. What is sin? How do Christians think it can be dealt with?

2. Relate some of the historical events, as Jews and Christians tell of them, in God's attempt to re-establish his Kingdom among humans after they broke away in sinful disobedience.

3. What sort of love do Christians recommend, and what is it modeled on? Give several examples.

CHAPTER 10
AUGUSTINE
God and the Soul

ESSENTIAL POINTS

- Early years
  - Incident of the pears: pride as an attempt to be God
  - Love of wisdom
  - The problem of evil
  - The attractions of Manicheanism; his disillusionment with it
  - Ambrosian Christianity
  - Conversion
- Wisdom, Happiness, and God
  - Faith seeking understanding
  - Happiness as getting what wisdom approves
  - Refuting skepticism; the reality of truth
  - Argument that God exists
- The Interior Teacher
  - All are enlightened by the *logos,* who is Christ
  - The resources of Greek philosophy used to help understand Christian teaching
  - We do not learn from words, but by confronting realities, illuminated by the inner light
- God and the World
  - The Great Chain of Being
    — Plotinus and emanation from the One
    — Creation
    — Degrees of being and goodness correlate
  - Evil is not a reality, but a privation of being
  - The puzzle of time and God's eternity
- Human Nature and Its Corruption
  - The soul as a substance whose function is to rule the body
  - Sin is a disordered love life; our loves involve the consent of the will
  - There is no positive cause for sin; the will is free and we are responsible
  - Pride is the essence of sin
  - God's foreknowledge is not incompatible with free will

- Human Nature and Its Restoration
  * We cannot make ourselves whole
  * Faith is a response, in gratitude, to God's grace
  * Using created goods and enjoying God
  * Contrast with "trading-skill religion"
  * Charity and cupidity
- Augustine on Relativism
  * The relevance of motivation and circumstances in judging right and wrong
  * The absoluteness of love and the relativity of action
- The Two Cities
  * Earthly and heavenly city have the same goal: peace
  * Distinguished by two kinds of love
  * The twofold citizenship of members of the City of God
- Christians and Philosophers
  * The importance of reason but the superiority of authority
  * Will is deeper than intellect
  * The self-indulgence of Epicureans and the pride of the Stoics

TEACHING SUGGESTIONS

1.   Augustine is a particularly "existential" thinker, concerned from first to last with the nature of human life and its problems. Beginning students often find Augustine a sympathetic figure and an accessible route into philosophical problems. Perhaps a contrast with his antithesis, Nietzsche (Chapter 20), would be especially stimulating.

2.   Students need to understand that "charity," as Augustine uses the term, is not simply a matter of giving to the needy. It is an orientation of the will that affects all of life.

3.   I have sometimes begun the discussion of Augustine's view of human corruption with a long list of evils taken from the daily papers and news programs. It is easy to make such a list. After contemplating the list for a few minutes, I ask, "What's wrong with us? Why is it so *easy* to make such a long list of evils?"

EXAM QUESTIONS
A. Multiple-Choice Questions

1. Augustine claims to be able to refute skepticism by
    a. arguing that God would not deceive us.
    x b. showing that the supposition that we could be mistaken about everything is absurd.
    c. pursuing that skeptical infinite regress right to its end.
    d. a direct appeal to Christ, the Interior Teacher.

2. Augustine
    a. agrees with Socrates that virtue is knowledge.
    b. agrees with Socrates that the explanation for wrong-doing is ignorance.
    x c. agrees with St. Paul that our wills are divided and that we cannot heal ourselves.
    d. agrees that the self-reliance of the Stoics is the key to happiness.

3. Augustine was attracted to the Manicheans because they
    x a. seemed to deal with the problem of evil in a rational manner.
    b. held that there is one God, omnipotent, omniscient, and perfectly good.
    c. took the scriptures literally.
    d. thought, as Augustine himself did, that will was more fundamental than intellect.

4. Augustine solves the problem of natural evil by
    a. feeding the hungry and providing for the poor.
    b. accepting that there is, always has been, and always will be an evil power in conflict with the good.
    c. arguing that without evil there couldn't be any good.
    x d. denying that evil is a positive reality.

5. One crucial step in Augustine's argument that God must exist is this:

     a. Truth exists and is superior to all.
     b. Whatever is superior to us is God.
   x c. Either nothing is superior to truth or there is something superior to truth.
     d. As the measure of all that is and of all that is not, there is nothing superior to us.

6. Unlike Plotinus, Augustine holds that

     a. all of being streams incessantly in an eternal emanation from the One.
   x b. the created world is not continuous with the being of God.
     c. worldly things differ from each other in both being and goodness.
     d. all that is arises mysteriously out of the primal nothingness.

7. In meditating on the puzzling nature of time, Augustine concludes that

     a. time is an illusion and only God's eternity exists.
     b. neither the past nor the future nor the present can have any reality at all.
   x c. time came into being with the creation.
     d. God endures through all past and future time, as well as in the present.

8. Sin, according to Augustine, is

   x a. having a disordered love life.
     b. not to be attributed to babies, who are truly innocent.
     c. something that just happens to us—a fate we cannot help.
     d. a mistake we make when we don't know better.

9. Why do we sin? Augustine answers that
   a. we were created with a flaw that tends toward evil.
   b. we are made to sin by the Evil One, who tempts us and
      leads us into evil.
   x c. there is no cause for it.
   d. it is because we have a body dragging us down from the
      spiritual plane.

10. A good and happy life, Augustine thinks, is
   a. the result of an act of free will that straightens out our
      disordered loves.
   b. one of those things that is in our power, as opposed to
      things not in our power.
   x c. the result of God's grace.
   d. reached by identifying yourself with the pure, unsullied
      soul within.

11. Citizens of the heavenly city
   x a. have a dual citizenship.
   b. live lives of quiet perfection, in contrast to the citizens of
      the earthly city.
   c. pursue peace, in contrast to the citizens of the earthly city.
   d. are those who have died and gone to heaven.

B. Short-Answer Questions

1. What insight into human nature does Augustine draw from the
incident of stealing the pears?
   He concludes that we long to exercise a prerogative that rightly belongs
to God alone—to be in a position to *decide* what is good and what is evil. We are
attracted to breaking the law out of pride, our desire (will) not to conform to what is
laid down as good, but to be in control of good and evil.

2. Why does Augustine think that will is deeper in us than intellect?
   Will is deeper than intellect, he thinks, because unless our will is rightly
directed, we will not even be able to understand the truth, let alone accept it, when
it is present before us. We need to *want* to be open to the truth if our intellect is to
do its proper job.

3. What is Augustine's argument against the Skeptics?

I *cannot* suspend judgment about everything. For instance, let me suppose that I am mistaken about the fact that I exist. But if I am mistaken about it—or anything at all—then I must exist. For if I do not exist, how could I be mistaken, or suspend judgment, or do anything? So I do know something—namely, that I exist. So the Skeptics must be wrong.

4. State "the problem of evil."

If God is perfectly good, all-powerful, and infinitely wise, then there would not be any evil. But there is evil. So either God is not good (does not wish to remove the evil), not powerful enough to remove it, or doesn't know about it—or some combination of the three.

5. Explain the idea of the Great Chain of Being.

Reality comes in degrees. Some things that exist simply have more *being* than other things; there is more to them, more capacity, more power. Beings can be arranged on a kind of chain, from greater to lesser, from God at the top (HE WHO IS—i.e., pure being itself) down to nothingness. This chain is also a ladder of value or goodness, since BEING = GOODNESS. The more being the more good. So God is perfectly good, and all of creation good, but not as good as God. Humans were made to be somewhere in the middle of this chain.

6. How does the notion of the Great Chain of Being help Augustine to solve the problem of evil?

The chain shows us that creation must have less being (and therefore less goodness) than God—or it would be identical with God. It stretches in a continuum from the best created things to absolute nothingness. Evil is not a positive reality but simply the absence (lack, privation) of good. So God did not create it. Whatever is—insofar as it *is*—is good, although not perfectly good, or it would simply be God.

7. What is the puzzle about measuring time, and how does Augustine solve it?

How can we measure time, or think of a "long time," since the past is no longer, the future is not yet, and the present has no temporal extension. Where is this "long time"? He resolves the puzzle by holding that the past should really be understood to be a present—a present of things past (memory)—and the future also a present—a present of things to come (expectation). So we measure time in our minds—in memory and expectation.

8. The Manichees had asked, derisively, "What do you Christians say God was doing before he created heaven and earth?" What is Augustine's answer?

The question contains a mistaken presupposition—that before heaven and earth were created there *was* a "before." Time, as a measure of motion and change, came into being along with the created world. So "before" there was a world, there was no time. And the question makes no sense. God exists not "everlastingly," but "eternally," atemporally, in an eternal NOW.

9. Why, according to Augustine, is sin more than just a mistake?

Sin is not just a mistake because we cooperate in it, we accede to it, assent to it—in short, because we will it. Sin is not something that *happens* to us. If we look for a cause to explain sin, we will find nothing; looking for a cause (a reality) to account for sin is like trying to see darkness or hear silence. There is no cause. We sin freely.

10. Why did God make creatures that could sin, that could do such terrible things as humans do?

God made creatures who were capable of sinning because that is the only way he could make creatures capable of goodness or virtue. No one is righteous who cannot choose to be righteous. But that requires free will. And creatures with free will can also go wrong.

11. Explain Augustine's concept of the "two cities." What do they have in common, and how do they differ?

The City of God and the City of Man, the heavenly and the earthly cities, have the same goal: peace. But the citizens of the earthly city try to arrange that peace for themselves, on their own terms, and fall prey to pride. Greed, envy, and conflict result. Citizens of the heavenly city are like resident aliens here on earth, knowing that peace can be experienced fully only beyond life. Unlike the earthly citizens, they do not settle down to *enjoy* the relative goods that the world affords; nonetheless, they value such peace as politics can afford and are willing to cooperate in producing it. Basically, the two cities are distinguished by their loves, by cupidity on the one hand and charity on the other.

12. In terms of enjoyment and use, charity and cupidity, explain how Augustine thinks of the good life for human beings.

Only God is to be enjoyed for himself, or absolutely; other things only as relatively good benefits bestowed by God. The things of this world are to be used to bring ourselves and others closer to God.

Charity is ordered love—loving things according to their actual value (their position on the Great Chain of Being). Cupidity is disordered love—loving more what should be loved less and less what should be loved more. So cupidity is directed to things of less value as though they were worth more than they really are. Charity relates to all things in an appropriate way.

The good life, then, is a life in which our loves are ordered appropriately, according to the degrees of goodness in things. It is a life of charity, of ordered love. If our loves are rightly ordered, Augustine can say, "Love—and do what you like."

13. Sketch Augustine's argument for the existence of God.

God is, by definition, that to which nothing is superior. We wonder: is there anything superior to ourselves? And we answer: Of course; truth is superior to ourselves, since we are not the judge of it, or the creator of it; truth must be *acknowledged*. Now, either there is nothing superior to truth, or there is something superior to truth. In the first case, truth exists and truth is God. In the second case, whatever is superior to truth is God. In either case, God exists.

14. Explain Augustine's saying, "Love and do what you will." What does he mean by "love," and what kind of love is he talking about?

A love is a desire—delighting in the possession of something. The sort of love that allows you to do whatever you want is *charity*—ordered love, loving God above all other things (as is fitting for the perfect source of all being and goodness), our neighbors as ourselves (as is fitting for beings at the same level on the Chain), and everything else in accord with its true value. If love like that could fill our hearts, whatever we wanted to do would be OK.

EXTRA CREDIT QUESTION: In Augustine's view, our experience of time is both like and unlike God's. Compare the two, bringing in also what must be (we imagine) the temporal experience of, say, an oyster. Show how these experiences all fit into the Great Chain of Being.

God exists "outside" of time altogether; he sees everything—past, present, and future—in an instant, in a great eternal NOW. Our time sense is more limited. Yet we are not altogether immersed in time either. Like God, we can know the past (by remembering it—in the present), the future (by expecting it—in the present), and the present (by being present to it—in the present).

An oyster, we suppose, has no such expansive time consciousness. It has a very narrow window open to time, existing without much in the way of either memory or expectation. We are higher on the Great Chain because we have more being (and value) than the oyster, in part because of our capacities with respect to time. So God is at the top of the Chain, we, somewhere near the middle, and the oyster, considerably lower.

C. Essay Questions

1. In terms of what Augustine calls "loves," discuss what is wrong with human beings and what a good life would consist of.

2. Discuss Augustine's concept of God and of God's relation to the rest of reality.

3. Imagine that Democritus (the atomist) and Augustine are discussing the nature of ultimate reality. Write a brief dialogue in which they express and argue for their views on this matter.

4. Imagine that Heraclitus, Socrates, Plato, Aristotle, Epictetus (the Stoic), Epicurus (the Hedonist), and Augustine have been having a debate about the good life for a human being. The debate is about to come to an end and each is asked to make a brief final statement summing up what he believes about this important issue. Here is what each says:

CHAPTER 11
ANSELM AND AQUINAS
Existence and Essence in God and the World

ESSENTIAL POINTS

- Anselm
  * The definition of God as that than which no greater can be conceived; its justification
  * The argument, in some detail
  * What kind of fool is it that says there is no God
  * How the concepts of essence and existence are used in the argument
  * Gaunilo and the objection from the idea of a perfect island; Anselm's reply
- Aquinas
  * Reason and faith complement each other
  * Review of the essentials of Aristotelian metaphysics accepted by Aquinas
  * Existence is something added to the essence of created substances, which includes both form and matter
  * We are not in the right position to make use of Anselm's argument, since we do not have a direct intuition of the essence of God
  * The "five ways" of proving God's existence
  * God is fundamentally being itself
  * Analogy as the key to knowledge of God's nature
  * Humans are unitary beings, governed by rationality—yet they have immortal souls
  * Human knowledge
    — Begins in the senses
    — Makes use of universal concepts abstracted from particulars
    — Represents things in the world independent of ourselves
  * Human good
    — *Eudaemonia* as the end
    — Means to that end are chosen by acts of will informed by reason

- Good acts are those that flow from our nature as rational creatures
- The natural law as God's reason embedded in creation
- Human law: its four conditions
- Virtues as habits of character formed by practice and oriented toward blessedness
- The final blessedness of eternal life
- Ockham and Skeptical Doubts—Again
  * The impact of the condemnation of heretical opinions
  * Omnipotence is the power to do whatever is possible
  * Ockham's argument, based on God's omnipotence, against certainty

TEACHING SUGGESTIONS

1. The continuing importance of the basic outlooks of Plato and Aristotle can be illustrated through a comparison of Augustine and Aquinas, both Christians, but different in so many ways.

2. After students have understood the proofs for God's existence in this chapter, you might ask them to choose one proof and write a half-page to a full page on it by way of critique. Your evaluations of their criticisms should be a useful learning experience for them.

EXAM QUESTIONS
A. Multiple-Choice Questions

1. Anselm's "ontological" argument for the existence of God
   a. begins with easily observed facts about the world.
   b. moves from the premise that I exist to the conclusion that God exists.
   x c. purports to establish that "There is no God" is self-contradictory.
   d. begins from the idea of God as the greatest thing I can conceive.

2. The fool who "says in his heart" that there is no God
   x a. believes that God doesn't exist and also that God does exist.
   b. is an impossibility, because being such a fool is self-contradictory.
   c. is obviously not thinking of God at all.
   d. could be correct but is mistaken according to Anselm.

3. Anselm's argument
   a. moves from existence to essence.
   b. presupposes that God exists.
   x c. starts from essence and ends with existence.
   d. begins with premises derived from Christian faith.

4. Thomas Aquinas
   a. depends on Anselm's ontological argument to buttress faith with reason.
   b. rejects Anselm's argument as invalid.
   c. thinks that God's existence cannot be proved but must be accepted on faith.
   x d. holds that we are not in the right epistemological position to use Anselm's argument.

5. Reason and revelation, Aquinas holds,
   a. are irreconcilably in conflict.
   x b. are two compatible sources of truth.
   c. cannot deal with the same topics.
   d. both depend on faith for their validation.

6. Existence, Aquinas tells us,
   a. is included in form, the principle of actuality in things.
   b. is something we can take for granted.
   x c. is something added to the essence of finite things.
   d. derives from essence, and from essence alone.

7. The argument for God's existence from motion
   a. claims that every change is a transition from actuality to potentiality.
   b. assumes that something can be simultaneously both potentially hot and actually hot.
   c. assumes that changes can be traced back to infinity.
   x d. argues that without a first mover there would be no intermediate movers.

8. In the argument from possibility and necessity, Aquinas reasons that
   a. since at one time nothing existed, something must have come from nothing.
   x b. not every being could be a merely possible being.
   c. every being is a necessary being; otherwise, there would be an infinite regress.
   d. some necessary beings have their being caused by merely possible beings.

9. We cannot know, Aquinas says,
   a. anything about God's nature, because all our knowledge begins in sense experience.
   b. that God's very substance is being itself.
   c. that God is the cause of the world.
   x d. what the nature of God is through direct acquaintance.

10. Aquinas says that a human soul
   x a. is the form of a human body.
   b. inhabits the body like a sailor his ship.
   c. is potentially a human being.
   d. is the substance of a human being, which in turn is a composite of form and matter.

11. What we know first and most easily, according to Aquinas,
   a. is the soul.
   b. are the contents of our own minds.
   x c. are things like carrots and clouds.
   d. are ideas of things like carrots and clouds.

12. What is right for us to do, according to natural law,
    a. can be known only through careful attention to what is described as natural in the scriptures.
    b. is whatever naturally feels right.
    c. is whatever God, the author of nature, arbitrarily legislates as right.
  x d. expresses our nature as rational human beings.

B. Short-Answer Questions

1. The atheist says, "There is no God." Imagine you are Anselm. What can you say to him or her?

Don't be a fool. If you understand what is meant by the term "God," that God is that, than which no greater can be conceived, you must see that God exists. For suppose he doesn't. Then that, than which no greater can be conceived, would exist only in your mind and not also in reality. But then it wouldn't be that, than which no greater can be conceived. So to say that God does not exist involves you in contradictions. You can't consistently even *think* that. So don't be such a fool.

2. Why does Thomas Aquinas think we cannot use Anselm's argument?

Aquinas says that Anselm's argument takes it to be self-evident that God exists. That is, from the very conception of God (without knowing anything else), we should be able to conclude that God exists. Or, to put it another way, that we can see that God's existence is part of his very essence—*that* God is follows necessarily from *what* God is. But this presupposes that we have an intellectual intuition into the essence of God.

Aquinas says, however (following Aristotle), that our minds operate on materials presented to us by our senses. And so we cannot assume we have an adequate grasp of God's essence. Anselm's argument may be correct, but we are not in the right epistemological situation to see that it is. So we have to argue another way.

3. What is the relation between reason and revelation, according to Aquinas?

Human reason and experience can lead us to the truth on many issues, even though humans are subject to sin. Revelation builds on reason but does not contradict it. Some things are knowable through reason that are also revealed—such as the existence of God. Other things we know only because God has

74

revealed them—such as the fact that Christ is the incarnation of the second person of the Trinity. But even such truths do not contradict reason, for God himself is the very source of reason.

4. How are essence and existence related in finite creatures, according to Aquinas?

The essence of material things includes both their form and their matter, but not their existence. Existence—if they have it—is something added by God. Spiritual substances like the angels contain no matter, but they too are composite, existence again being something not included in their form. You can understand the essence of any created thing without understanding that it exists.

[Students may be asked to give the essentials of any of the five ways of proving God's existence.]

5. Where do the words that we use to talk about God get their meaning, since we are not directly acquainted with God?

Aquinas says that we are entitled to use terms for God that come from our experience of the world, since God is the cause of the world and everything in it. When we use such terms, however, we need to be aware that we are not using them univocally, but by analogy or proportion. Words used of God, then, are used metaphorically and borrow their original meaning from things with which we are acquainted.

6. According to Aquinas, am I identical with my soul?

No, I am a human being, a rational animal. My soul is the form of my body, which is the matter for this form, making up, along with existence, the substance that I am. Neither the body nor the soul is an independent substance, but only the human being that I am.

7. In what sense is a human will free?

Unlike the lower animals who directly act out of their desires and the circumstances they are in, humans can consider those desires and circumstances in terms of concepts or universals. They can also contemplate alternatives to acting on those desires. So they are not closely determined by the desires and circumstances but can take thought as to whether to act on such a desire or not. Acting on a desire in the light of rational reflection is what Aquinas understands by an act of will. Our will is free in the sense that we are able to decide whether to act on a desire.

8. What are virtues, and why are they useful to us?

A virtue is a habit of choosing wisely in the light of our ultimate desire to be happy or blessed. They are useful to us because our desires and emotions have a certain independence of reason and, if unrestrained, are likely to lead us to do things that will frustrate our ultimate end. Virtues, then, bring our impulses and inclinations under the direction of reason.

9. Is the fact that God cannot make a cube with seven sides a limitation on his power? Explain.

It is true that God cannot make a cube with seven sides, but this is no limitation on his power. The only thing that would limit God's omnipotence would be his inability to do something that is *possible* to do. But seven-sided cubes are impossible. There is nothing there that might or might not be done. Omnipotence is the ability to do anything possible.

10. How does reflecting on God's omnipotence tend to undermine the premises of Aquinas' arguments?

All of Aquinas' arguments begin with something he says we know via the senses (change, causality, coming to be and passing away...). But it is *possible* that God should create *only* the mental representations of those things and not the things themselves. And God can do anything that is possible. So the sort of religious certainty wanted for the *conclusion* of these arguments (that God exists) is lacking in the first *premise*. So the arguments cannot guarantee the truth of the conclusion.

C. Essay Questions

1. Compare the kind of argument that Anselm puts forward with the kind that Aquinas favors. What are the significant differences? Why do those differences exist?

2. Aquinas relies heavily upon Aristotle for many basic concepts and principles. Where does he differ, and why?

3. Choose one of the five ways Aquinas thinks God's existence can be proved and criticize the argument.

CHAPTER 12
MOVING FROM MEDIEVAL TO MODERN

ESSENTIAL POINTS

- The World God Made for Man
    * Finite, earth-centered, governed by final causes, celestial spheres quite different from earth; the stage for the drama of humanity
    * Dante and the integration of religious meaning with physical fact
- The Humanists
    * Inspired by the recovery of the classics
    * Celebrating human potentiality and the possibility of perfection
- Reforming the Church
    * Corruption; indulgences as an example
    * Luther's personal struggle; discovery of God's grace
    * The conflict between criteria for truth
- Skeptical Thoughts Revived
    * The odd nature of Montaigne's "defense" of Raymond Sebond
    * The consequences of skepticism for one's life choices
- Copernicus to Kepler to Galileo: the revolution in world view made possible by the new science (see below for contrasts)

TEACHING SUGGESTIONS

1.   This chapter is transitional, and I do not spend a lot of teaching time on it. It is interesting in its own right, of course, but has the function here of setting up the problems that "modern" philosophy will be dealing with.

2.   I find it useful to make a two-column list, contrasting the old medieval way of looking at the world with the newer picture of things. For example:

OLD: The universe is thought to be finite.
NEW: The universe is thought to be infinite.
OLD: The earth is in the center.

NEW: There is no center.

OLD: Celestial matter quite different from terrestrial.

NEW: Matter and motion are uniform throughout the universe.

OLD: Everything has its place.

NEW: Neutral space supplants meaningful places.

OLD: Everything has its purpose, its final cause.

NEW: Final causes are banished in favor of mathematical formulas describing how things occur.

OLD: The universe is stage-setting for its central drama: human sin and salvation.

NEW: It becomes less easy to believe that it all exists for us.

OLD: Things have the qualities they seem to have; fire is yellow and hot.

NEW: Secondary qualities become subjective effects of purely quantitative entities.

Such a list sets up nicely the problems Descartes struggles with, as he tries to integrate the new picture of things with human concerns about God, the soul, and free will.

EXAM QUESTIONS
A. Multiple-Choice Questions

1. In the Aristotle-Ptolemy-Dante picture of the world,
   x a. heaven is understood to be quite literally up above us.
   b. space is thought to be infinite.
   c. the sun is located in the very center of the created universe.
   d. human beings are thought to be insignificant in comparison with the glories of the celestial bodies.

2. Renaissance humanists
   a. intensify the otherworldliness embedded in medieval culture by emphasizing that human perfection is possible only in the life to come.
   b. see clearly that a good human life, as represented in the classics, is incompatible with Christianity.
   x c. celebrate the human being as the central fact in all the created world.
   d. tend to be pessimistic about humanity's prospects.

3. Martin Luther
   a. speaks of man as "maker and molder" of himself.
   b. upholds the Church as the legitimate interpreter of scripture, lest chaos result from individual opinions.
   c. leaves the Church, resigning his priesthood in disgust over the selling of indulgences.
   x d. stresses the grace of God and the inability of human beings to save themselves.

4. In defending the theology of Raymond Sebond, Montaigne
   a. shows that Sebond's arguments are superior to the arguments of those who criticized him.
   b. makes use of Plato's Forms to show that God is knowable to us.
   c. relies on Aristotle as the authority who showed us how to avoid infinite regress problems.
   x d. says only that Sebond's arguments are as solid and firm as any.

5. The new science
   x a. seems to require a distinction between primary and secondary qualities.
   b. shows how final causes actually work.
   c. puts the sun in the center of the universe.
   d. finally solves the old philosophical problems about knowledge.

B. Short-Answer Questions

1. Where is hell, in the picture Dante gives us, and what do the various circles of hell represent?

Hell is located inside the earth. The circles contain sinners of various kinds and degrees of seriousness, the worst sinners further toward the bottom. In each circle the unrepentant sinners suffer punishments appropriate to their sins.

2. What does Pico della Mirandola mean when he says that man is created as "maker and molder" of himself?

Human beings do not have a given nature, as do other things in the created world. We are made indeterminate and can be anything we want to be. For this purpose we were given a free will, which distinguishes us decisively from other things.

3. What is the disagreement between Luther and the Church basically about?

The heart of it is not indulgences or corruption, but authority. To what authority should the Christian look in deciding matters of faith and life? Luther points to the Bible as the original record of God's revelation. The Church agrees, but says it must be properly interpreted, and that is the job of the Church. So they are engaged in an argument about the correct criterion for judgments about truth and goodness.

4. How does Montaigne "defend" the claim of Raymond Sebond to rationally demonstrate all the doctrines of Christianity?

Montaigne uses skeptical arguments (e.g., infinite regress, circular reasoning, criterion problems of various kinds) to try to show us that Sebond's arguments for Christian doctrine are every bit as good as the arguments of his opponents—that is, none of them are any good at all.

5. Explain Galileo's distinction between primary and secondary qualities.

The real, or primary, properties of things are shape, size, weight, velocity, and so on—the sorts of things a mechanistic physics can explain. We are mistaken to attribute qualities such as color, warmth, and smell to them. These are secondary qualities, produced in us by the action of the primary qualities of things on our senses.

C. Essay Question

Compare, in as many ways as you can, the new scientific picture of the world with the older medieval view.

CHAPTER 13
RENÉ DESCARTES
Doubting Our Way to Certainty

ESSENTIAL POINTS

- The discovery of analytic geometry: how it fashions his intellectual style
- Descartes' science: geometry as the key
- The Method
  * The four rules
  * Their application to philosophical problems: his determination to accept nothing that can be doubted
- *Meditations*
  * Their purpose: to establish once and for all a foundation for knowing the external world, via proving the existence and nature of God and the soul
  * The metaphysical inventory
  * *Meditation I*
    — Three stages of skepticism: sensory illusions, dreams, the demon deceiver
    — Wiping the slate clean
  * *Meditation II*
    — The attractions of the representational theory, and how it naturally leads to skepticism
    — The cogito: how it satisfies the rules of method by being something simple and indubitable
    — The bit of wax and the hats and coats; the moral: whatever is known we know through the intellect, not through the senses
  * *Meditation III*
    — Solving the problem of the criterion
    — The inventory of the contents of our minds; what innate ideas are, and how they are distinctive
    — Subjective vs. formal/eminent reality
    — The specter of solipsism
    — There are degrees of reality
    — The two arguments for God's reality
  * *Meditation IV*

- Error explained as will outreaching intellect
- How error can be avoided
* *Meditation V*
    - Material things are *essentially* extended volumes
    - The third proof for God's existence
* *Meditation VI*
    - Why material things *could* exist: they can be clearly and distinctly conceived
    - Conceiving is not imagining: the example of the chiliagon
    - The argument for the distinctness of soul from body
    - The argument for the reality of material things
    - The proper functions of the senses
    - Why God is justified in giving us senses that sometimes deceive

TEACHING SUGGESTIONS

1. It can be both fun and interesting to students to invite one up to have a dialogue with you—in which you essentially work through the argument of the first Meditation. You put something, an eraser, say, into his or her hand. "What is this?" "Are you sure?" "How do you know?" "Have your eyes ever deceived you?" "A dream?" "A powerful deceiver?" "Do you have a hand?" "An arm?" "A body?" "How do you know?"

Well, you can see how it might go. When it works well, the student is baffled, and the class amazed. A good introduction to Descartes.

2. In going over the text of the first Meditation, it is useful to pay close attention to Descartes' own hesitations and objections, emphasizing how *hard* it is to doubt and how natural to believe.

3. Students sometimes think that engaging in deception is a sign of power, not weakness, as Descartes says (in claiming that a God of infinite perfections would not deceive him). Reflection on their own experience can help them see that Descartes' point is at least not obviously wrong. When do they resort to deception? When they can't attain their ends directly, openly, honestly (at least, for the most part).

EXAM QUESTIONS
A. Multiple-Choice Questions

1. Among the rules of Descartes' method is the following:
    a. Doubt only what you have clear and distinct, conclusive reason for doubting.
    b. Multiply possibilities lest you miss a plausible alternative.
    c. Accept only what an authoritative source reveals.
    x d. Make comprehensive reviews.

2. In the Meditations, Descartes aims to
    a. establish the irrelevance of God to modern physics.
    b. show that the soul is identical with the body.
    x c. provide a firm foundation for knowledge.
    d. prove that first philosophy is founded on a mistake.

3. We ought to doubt our senses, Descartes says, because
    x a. they sometimes deceive us.
    b. we don't understand God's purposes.
    c. there exists an evil deceiver intent on leading us astray.
    d. we are dreaming.

4. On the representational theory,
    a. we have direct and immediate access to the world around us, as it is represented by our ideas.
    x b. what we know best are the ideas in our minds.
    c. we can tell which ideas represent things correctly by observing their causal conditions.
    d. things serve as representations of our ideas.

5. The result of Descartes' methodical doubt is that
    a. he knows nothing.
    b. he knows that he is a rational animal.
    c. he doubts his own existence.
    x d. he finds something that can indicate a criterion for knowledge.

6. What Descartes calls the "light of nature"
   x a. certifies something as true because it is lighted up as so clear and distinct it cannot be doubted.
   b. is the same as what is "taught by nature."
   c. is known innately as revealed to us by God.
   d. cannot be relied upon unless it is backed up by extensive argument, going back to simples and moving deliberately to complexes.

7. Innate ideas, according to Descartes, are
   a. what every infant already possesses by inheritance.
   b. what everyone comes to have by virtue of common human experience.
   c. ideas composed by us out of other ideas.
   x d. ideas I would have even if nothing but I existed.

8. Descartes' first argument for God's existence, in Meditation III,
   x a. is a causal argument.
   b. moves directly from the idea of God to God's existence.
   c. relies on the principle that everything must originally have come from nothing.
   d. uses the idea that there must be an infinite regress to guarantee infinite perfection.

9. Why, after proving God's existence, does human error become a problem for Descartes?
   a. Because we might have made a mistake in the proof.
   b. Because we know our senses sometimes deceive us.
   x c. Because we know God is perfect and wouldn't deceive us.
   d. Because it's always a problem to discriminate error from the truth.

10. The essence of material things, according to Descartes, is
    x a. extendedness.
    b. externality to the mind.
    c. existence.
    d. solidity.

11. Descartes argues that material things exist, by
    a. pointing out that not only can we see them, but we can touch them as well.
    b. relying on the fact that our senses do not *always* deceive us.
    c. showing that even if the evil demon deceives us, it still seems to us as though they do exist.
    x d. claiming that if they did not exist, God would be a deceiver.

12. Descartes thinks it is important to prove the existence of God because
    a. otherwise many people would not believe.
    b. you should not trust the scriptures to tell you the truth.
    x c. otherwise you couldn't be sure of anything but your own existence.
    d. it is an essential bulwark for a pious life.

B. Short-Answer Questions

1. State the four rules of Descartes' method, the method that he thinks will allow us to make intellectual progress.
    1. Do not accept anything unless it is so clear and distinct that it cannot be doubted.
    2. Analyze complex problems into their simple elements.
    3. Beginning with the simpler, construct solutions moving toward the more complex.
    4. Make comprehensive reviews, being sure nothing has been left out.

2. To what certainty does Descartes' methodical doubt lead? What makes him think he is right about that?
    To the certainty that he himself exists: *cogito ergo sum*. He thinks he must be right about that because it is so clear and distinct that he cannot possibly doubt it; if he tries to doubt it, he demonstrates its truth.

3. What qualities belong essentially to something like a bit of wax? Why?
    The wax is essentially an *extended thing*, having size, shape, volume, motion, duration. It has the qualities treatable in a mathematical physics. Many of the qualities that our senses attribute to the wax can change, while the wax

remains the same thing; moreover, it can go through more changes (an infinite number) than our senses can detect. So material things must be understood by the intellect alone.

4.   What is the problem of the criterion? And how does Descartes think he is, after Meditation II, in a position to solve that problem?

The problem of the criterion has to do with the standard you appeal to in justifying a claim to know something: How do you know that is the right standard? This question can be repeated, so that it seems you are driven either into an infinite regress or a vicious circle. Descartes, after discovering the *cogito*, thinks he can bring the regress to an end and cut the circle, because in the *cogito* we do have certainty—knowledge of something self-evident, lighted up in itself by the light of nature. Because I know that I exist, anything with the same clarity and distinctness will also be known to be true. Clarity and distinctness, then, can serve as a criterion for truth.

5.   Why does Descartes feel a need to inquire about the existence and nature of God?

He knows that he exists but is doubtful of anything else. Threatened by solipsism, he needs to prove that he is not alone in the world. To do that, he needs to disprove the hypothesis of the demon deceiver, which he can do if he can show that an infinitely perfect being exists. Unless God's existence can be demonstrated, even his own physics cannot be shown to be more than a dream.

6.   Descartes distinguishes between what he is "taught by nature" and what "the light of nature" teaches him. Explain.

What he is taught by nature is what he has a spontaneous impulse to believe, what seems natural to accept, what he can hardly help believing. The light of nature, however, only teaches what is so clear and distinct that it cannot possibly be doubted.

7.   How does the conviction that God is not a deceiver help Descartes to establish the reality of an external, material world?

He has a nearly irresistible impulse to believe that his sensory experience is caused by real objects external to his mind—that when he seems to be perceiving a bit of wax in his hand, there really is a bit of wax there. If it were not so, then God (who made him) would constantly be deceiving him. But God, an infinitely perfect being, is no deceiver. Therefore, he can trust this impulse—take it as reliable. And so there must actually (formally) exist material things beyond his ideas of them.

8. How does the distinction between understanding and will explain the possibility of error?

Our understanding is limited, but our will is not. The will, a faculty of saying yes or no, of affirming or denying, can be exercised on beliefs that are anything but certain (clear and distinct). When we affirm something we have not clearly and distinctly conceived to be true, we fall into error.

9. What is the representational theory of knowledge and perception? And what problem does it face?

This is the theory holding that we directly know only our own perceptions (impressions, ideas, etc.). These mental items are supposed to represent objects independent of the mind. Knowledge of such correspondence must, however, be inferred on the basis of argument. The problem is that it is very hard in this way to justify bridging the gap between our ideas and what they are supposed to represent—so skepticism threatens.

10. Use Descartes' discussion of the phantom limb phenomenon to explain how he believes God's goodness is compatible with certain types of errors.

In the phantom limb phenomenon an amputee makes a mistake of a certain kind: He believes he still has the limb that has been amputated. Why does he believe this? Because the nerves in the brain that produce the sensations of having the limb can be stimulated between the limb and the brain even if there is no longer a limb, thus producing the same sensation as if the limb were still there. But this kind of error is compatible with the goodness of God, since it is for the best in most situations—the situations of the healthy body—that these sensations be produced in this way.

11. Harry Frankfurt, in a presidential address to the American Philosophical Association a few years ago, said that modern philosophy was born in anxiety. If you reflect on what you know of Descartes, what would you say he meant?

Doubt causes anxiety. When we doubt as Descartes does, we lose our confidence that we know anything at all. Our natural belief in the world's reality vanishes like smoke in the wind. So Descartes, after the doubts of the first Meditation, faces the twin problems of skepticism and solipsism.

12. What is the hypothesis of the evil demon? How does Descartes believe he can rule out that hypothesis?

Descartes imagines there might be an evil deceiver who is constantly putting false ideas in his mind—so that whatever he takes to be true is really false (no matter how sure of it he is). He thinks that hypothesis could be ruled out by a proof that God exists—that the power that created us is infinitely perfect and so wouldn't deceive us.

13. Define these terms briefly:
    a. Solipsism: the idea that I am the only person that exists
    b. Innate ideas: ideas that any mind would have regardless of whether anything else exists
    c. Formal reality: what actually exists, independent of anyone knowing it to exist

C. Essay Questions

1. Set down in outline form either of Descartes' two causal proofs for the existence of God.

2. How does Descartes argue for the independent existence of soul and body?

3. What is Descartes' argument for the reality of material things?

4. What problems does Descartes' work in philosophy set for future philosophical consideration?

CHAPTER 14
HOBBES, LOCKE, AND BERKELEY
Materialism and the Beginnings of Empiricism

ESSENTIAL POINTS

- Hobbes
    * Aspects of the new science accepted by Hobbes
    * Resolution and composition: the two phases of method
    * The mechanistic analysis of mind
    * Materialist or epiphenomenalis
    * Regulated thought, words, and definitions
    * Voluntary motions in the service of vital motions; will as the last appetite in deliberation
    * Pleasure as our natural end
    * The state of nature: war
    * Seeking peace while defending ourselves
    * The "contract" establishes a sovereign: its absolute character
- Locke
    * Aim: to understand our understanding—how it works, what materials it has to work with, and how far it can reach
    * Experience as the source of all our ideas
        — Ideas of sensation and ideas of reflection
        — Simple and complex ideas
        — Operations on ideas
    * Our idea of substance
        — A substratum, unknown and unknowable
        — The powers of substances
    * Our idea of the soul as clear as our idea of material substance
    * Our idea of personal identity founded in consciousness, especially in memory
    * Words stand for ideas in the mind
    * Abstract terms present nominal essences, not real essences
    * Knowledge as agreement and disagreement among ideas
        — The kinds of agreement and disagreement
        — Real existence known by intuition in our own case,

by demonstration in God's case, and by sensation
in the case of material things
* Representative government
— The state of nature and the natural law
— A "contract" to avoid people being judges in their
own case
— Property: a natural right
— Limited government responsible to the people
* Of toleration
— The distinct spheres of church and state
— Toleration as an essential means to civil peace
• Berkeley
* Berkeley as a defender of common sense what that means
* How the philosophers have violated common sense, and
thus furnished ammunition for skeptics and atheists
* Criticism of the doctrine of abstract ideas: they are inco-
herent
* Positive account of how general words (or ideas) work
* The existence of spirits; for the rest, *esse est percipi*
* The primary qualities of objects in the same boat with the
secondary
* Ideas into things
* God's perceiving of things as the guarantee of their objec-
tivity from our point of view

TEACHING SUGGESTIONS

1. Those who know something of work in artificial intelligence (AI) can usefully bring this into the discussion of Hobbes.
His view that reasoning is reckoning is cited, for instance, as a
forerunner of classical AI by John Haugeland in his *Artificial
Intelligence: The Very Idea* (Cambridge, MA: The MIT Press,
1985).

2. Locke's ideas on personal identity can be expanded on in
interesting ways by bringing to bear various thought experi-
ments concerning fission, teletransportation, brain transplants,
and so on, as developed by thinkers such as Derek Parfit,
Bernard Williams, John Perry, and Peter Unger.

3. Berkeley is always fun. He's so outrageous—and yet so persuasive. Use him to show students how much like play intellectual work can be.

EXAM QUESTIONS
A. Multiple-Choice Questions

1. According to Hobbes, human life
   a. represents a distinctive level of soul, quite different from the plant and animal levels.
   b. is just a motion of limbs.
   x c. doesn't differ in principle from the operations of a watch.
   d. ceases when the soul departs from the body.

2. With respect to the human mind and its relation to the body, Hobbes
   x a. is a metaphysical monist.
   b. is, unlike Descartes, a dualist.
   c. argues against epiphenomenalism.
   d. is, like Descartes, a dualist.

3. In a state of nature, Hobbes holds,
   a. people do many unjust things.
   b. there are no such things as good and evil.
   x c. people seek to maximize their pleasure and power.
   d. cooperation predominates, until society corrupts the natural goodness of individuals.

4. Hobbes thinks that a sovereign power
   a. exists pure and uncorrupted only in a state of nature.
   x b. is required to compel men to keep their agreements.
   c. must be such as to be under the control of the governed.
   d. should involve a separation of powers, as between king and parliament.

5. When Locke says that he will use a "historical, plain method" in investigating human understanding, he means that he
    a. will consult the historians as authorities on humanity.
    b. won't say anything fancy.
  x c. will try to trace our ideas to their origin.
    d. throw out any "results" that cannot be validated historically.

6. All our ideas come from experience, Locke says—that is, from
  x a. sensation and reflection.
    b. innate sources of experience.
    c. complex ideas of external objects.
    d. within the mind.

7. Our idea of substance, Locke says, is
    a. the known foundation of all our knowledge of things.
    b. the idea of a composite of qualities that regularly appears together in our experience.
    c. restricted to the substance we know best, that is, our own soul.
  x d. the idea of an unknown substratum that has the qualities we experience.

8. The problem of personal identity, if Locke is right,
    a. is not a real problem at all, because we know who we are.
    b. can be solved by paying close attention to what is present to our consciousness at a given moment.
  x c. arises because a person can have such different qualities at different times.
    d. is solved by appeal to the sameness of the soul that constitutes the person.

9. Locke's views on representative government
  x a. are formed in part by his views on what life is like in a state of nature.
    b. depend on the contract signed between Englishmen and their king.
    c. involve no limitation on the powers of the sovereign, once he or she is constituted monarch.
    d. guarantee that government will not abuse its powers.

10. Berkeley thinks that
    a. philosophers have erred in trying to stick too close to common sense.
    b. philosophers have erred in trying to defend skepticism and atheism.
 x c. things really do have the qualities they seem to have.
    d. things do not exist independently of our perception of them.

11. Berkeley thinks that the doctrine of abstract ideas
    a. has led to many substantial advances in knowledge.
 x b. is one of the confusions that leads to atheism.
    c. is required to account for our knowledge of substances, particularly our knowledge of God.
    d. helps us understand how one mind can communicate its ideas to another mind via language.

12. Berkeley says that it is his intention to
 x a. turn ideas into things.
    b. turn things into ideas.
    c. make a significant advance on common sense.
    d. raise a dust and then complain he cannot see.

B. Short-Answer Questions

1. How does Hobbes explain thinking—particularly the difference between unregulated and regulated thinking?

All thought originates in sensation—that is, in the effect external objects have on our senses. These effects leave traces in us that, especially when structured by words, succeed one another according to rules. In unregulated thought such as idle daydreaming, the rules are those of customary associations. When regulated by desire seeking means to its satisfaction, thought becomes reasoning.

2. Why does Hobbes think life in a state of nature is "solitary, poor, nasty, brutish, and short"?

Because humans are egoistic hedonists, each seeking to maximize his or her own pleasure, together with enough power to secure continued enjoyment. As a result, humans are competitors, and the state of nature is a state of war—of "all against all."

93

3. Why does Hobbes think the establishment of a social contract demands a "coercive power"—that is, a sovereign?

Because individuals will have no good reason to trust each other to mutually limit their liberty unless there is a power to force them to keep their word. Since they are egoistic pleasure-seekers, they will take an opportunity to break the contract when it is to their advantage, if it is not clear that it will be against their interest to do so. That's what a sovereign can guarantee.

4. What does Hobbes mean when he speaks of a "law" of nature and a "right" of nature? Give an example of each.

A law of nature is simply a description of how things proceed. So when Hobbes says that the first law of nature is to seek peace, he means that a prudent individual in the state of nature will naturally come to see that this is what is required to secure his or her life and happiness. A right of nature, correspondingly, would be whatever a prudent person would do to preserve and defend his or her own life.

5. What, according to Locke, is the origin of all our ideas? And how does he understand that?

Locke says all our ideas originate in experience. There are no innate ideas. There are two sources: sensation—the experience of external objects through our senses, and reflection—ideas obtained by reflecting on our own mental operations.

6. What is the origin of our idea of substance, according to Locke?

We notice that in our experience some qualities regularly appear together. It seems implausible that this could be an accident, so we suppose there must be something that has these qualities. That substratum in which qualities have their being, we call substance. We never experience substances directly, and so have no proper idea of substances nor knowledge of their natures.

7. In what does personal identity consist, according to Locke? And in what does it not consist?

It does not consist in sameness of substance, whether of body or soul. Rather, it is founded in consciousness and, in particular, in memory. What makes me the same person as I was last year is my consciousness of the events in my life at that time. It would make no difference if either soul or body had changed in substance between then and now.

8. What is a nominal essence, what does Locke contrast it with, and how does he make use of this idea?

A nominal essence is an abstract idea attached to a general name, like "tiger." We create these nominal essences from our experiences of similarities in things. Because they are our creations, nominal essences must not be assumed to match perfectly the real essences of things. Things, which are always particular, do have real essences, but they are unknown to us. So the idea of a nominal essence is important in Locke's program of urging us to be modest in our claims to know.

9. What sort of government does Locke believe a social contract would reasonably create?

It would be a government of limited powers—simply enough to rectify the "inconveniences" in a state of nature. It would restrain the partiality and violence of men and guarantee people security in the enjoyment of their property. It will be responsible to the people who established it and incorporate a separation of legislative and executive powers. If it failed to provide for the safety and security of its citizens, they could rightly change it.

10. What is Berkeley's critique of abstract ideas?

Abstract ideas are supposed to be acquired by focusing only on those features of a thing it has in common with others of its kind. But that would produce incoherence: an idea of an oak tree that is neither young, nor old, neither tall nor short—and yet encompassing all of these qualities. So there cannot be such ideas.

11. How does Berkeley attack the idea that while secondary qualities exist only in being perceived, primary qualities are in things independently of perception?

He shows that exactly the same reasons for the mind-relativity of secondary qualities apply to primary qualities. They, too, vary with the conditions of perception. And if "to be is to be perceived" works for the former, it must apply to the latter as well.

12. Does Berkeley deny the existence of material substances?

If by "material substance" you mean what our experience gives us reason to affirm, then no, Berkeley does not deny that. But if you mean what the philosophers have meant by material substance—the unknowable substratum underlying all the perceptible qualities that ordinarily appear together—then, yes, he does deny that. But that, he thinks, is no loss, as the idea of such a thing rests on the confused notion of abstract ideas and is unintelligible in any case.

13. What role does God play in Berkeley's philosophy?

In addition to the usual religious functions—Berkeley was a bishop, after all—God functions as the guarantee of independence for things perceived by us. They do have their being in being perceived, but in being perceived by God, not by us. So they are not dependent on human perception of them.

C. Essay Questions

1. Contrast Descartes' view of the mind with that of Hobbes. Include a discussion of thinking, imagining, dreaming, and willing. Do not neglect any arguments offered by these philosophers on behalf of their beliefs.

2. Show how Locke's views about substance are informed by his convictions concerning how we get our ideas, together with his doctrine of abstract ideas.

3. Compare the views of Hobbes and Locke on life in a state of nature, together with the prescription each provides on how to get beyond its inconveniences.

4. Is Berkeley a critic of common sense, or its most consistent defender? Give reasons for thinking one thing or the other—or both.

5. What is Berkeley's argument for the conclusion that only spirits and their ideas exist?

6. What is Locke's view on abstract ideas? What is Berkeley's criticism of this view, and what does he recommend in its place?

CHAPTER 15
DAVID HUME
Unmasking the Pretensions of Reason

ESSENTIAL POINTS

- Enlightenment: Kant's account of it
- How Newton Did It
  * The method of analysis and synthesis
  * Newton frames no hypotheses but "deduces" conclusions from the phenomena
- To Be the Newton of Human Nature
  * Hume means to use Newtonian principles to understand human beings, especially their minds
  * He aims thereby to destroy superstition and dogmatism
- The Theory of Ideas
  * Ideas derived from impressions, complex ideas from simple
  * Hume's rule: to check a dubious idea, see whether it can be traced back to an impression
- The Association of Ideas
  * Ideas do not follow one another randomly
  * They are associated by contiguity, similarity, and cause and effect—the latter being the most important relation
- Causation: The Very Idea
  * Distinction: relations of ideas different from matters of fact
  * Cause and effect: the principle we make use of in knowing anything beyond the experience of the moment
  * How are causes known
    — Not through reasoning about the relations of ideas
    — By experience of constant conjunctions
    — The idea of necessary connection is a part of our idea of cause; that part is a fiction
    — That part supplied by a habit of expecting one thing when another occurs, based on previous experiences of constant conjunctions
    — The grounds of probability are to be found in looser connections between events

- The Disappearing Self
  * The traditional idea of the soul, spirit, or self
  * Trying to trace that idea back to an impression: there is no such impression
  * The self as a bundle of perceptions connected by association
- Rescuing Human Freedom
  * Hume can't take Descartes' way of preserving freedom
  * Clarifying the terms
    — That behavior is caused amounts simply to constant conjunctions
    — Liberty or freedom is hypothetical in nature
  * Freedom and lawful causation reconciled
- Is It Reasonable to Believe in God?
  * Critique of Descartes' first argument: I could originate the idea of God
  * Critique of Descartes' ontological argument: from relations of ideas, no truths about matters of fact can follow
  * Critique of the argument from design
- Understanding Morality
  * Reason alone never motivates an action
  * Passion is the motivator; reason is its slave
  * Morality is founded in sentiment
- Is Hume a Skeptic?
  * Antecedent and mitigated skepticism; the usefulness of the latter
  * Nature too strong for principle
  * Commit sophistry and illusion to the flames

TEACHING SUGGESTIONS

In teaching Hume on causation, I bring a tennis ball to class. Asking the students questions about what will happen if I throw it against the wall, whether they are sure, how they know, and asking them to describe very carefully what they observe when I do throw it—all this allows the points of Hume's analysis to be made in a lively and interactive way.

EXAM QUESTIONS
A. Multiple-Choice Questions

1. "Enlightenment," according to Kant, means
    a. relying only on the light of nature.
  x b. emergence from self-imposed immaturity.
    c. a capacity to empty the mind and receive divine light.
    d. having a book to serve as your understanding.

2. David Hume, prince of empiricists, thinks that
  x a. a science of human nature along Newtonian lines will be a strong defense against superstition.
    b. when we have an idea we are suspicious of, we should try to deduce it from an a priori principle.
    c. the succession of ideas in our minds is a result of necessary connections among them.
    d. our knowledge of causality is a matter of the *relations of ideas*.

3. Hume adopts Newton's motto, "frame no hypotheses," in order to
    a. restrict the foundations of our knowledge to innate ideas alone.
    b. avoid criticism by the defenders of traditional religion.
  x c. construct a science of human nature on the basis of the facts.
    d. defend religion from its attackers.

4. The idea of cause and effect, Hume thinks,
    a. is one of those a priori clear and distinct ideas that we can rely on in proving the existence of things that are the external causes of our ideas.
    b. embodies no idea of necessary connection between cause and effect.
  x c. is based on our experience of constant conjunctions between pairs of events.
    d. provides the bridge that gets us to things as they really are, independent of our impressions of them.

5. When Hume says that "all events seem entirely loose and separate," he means to imply that

     a. our experience of events is not to be trusted.

x b. there is no necessary connection to be observed among
       them.

     c. you can't really rely on anything.

     d. there is no constant conjunction of events to be discov-
       ered in the world.

6. Hume's view of the idea of the self is that it

     a. correctly represents what makes me the same person
       today as yesterday.

     b. is founded on an impression of a simple, unchanging sub-
       stance.

x c. is a fiction.

     d. is like a theater in being the permanent, unchanging thing
       that contains the ever-changing performance.

7. Hume thinks we can have both modern science and human
freedom. This is because

     a. the human soul escapes the network of scientific
       causality.

     b. modern science itself shows us that there are no laws of
       human behavior.

     c. we know God would not have created us as mere pup-
       pets.

x d. liberty and necessity, when properly understood, are seen
       to be compatible.

8. With regard to the existence of God, Hume says that
    a. there is no way I can be the originator of an idea of infinite perfection, since if I were, something would have come from nothing.
    b. the well-ordered character of the world proves a posteriori that the Author of Nature is somewhat similar to the mind of man.
  x c. revealed truth, together with philosophical skepticism, is the only sound basis for being a believer.
    d. the world was created by many wicked gods over a long time, during which they slowly gained skill in the art of world-making.

9. With regard to skepticism, Hume thinks that
  x a. a mitigated skepticism is a useful hedge against dogmatism and superstition.
    b. the skepticism of Descartes' first meditation strikes just the right note.
    c. once you go down the skeptical path, there is no recovery into a normal life.
    d. all human knowledge is just sophistry and illusion.

10. Value or moral judgments, according to Hume,
    a. are matters of fact and not relations of ideas.
  x b. are founded on sentiment or feeling.
    c. are based solely on self-interest.
    d. can be justified only by appeal to the authority of God.

B. Short-Answer Questions

1. According to Hume, what is the origin of our ideas? How does this view serve him in his critique of what he calls "superstition"?
    Ideas come from impressions. Hume recommends that when we have some doubt that an idea is genuine, we try to trace it back to the impression from which it originated. Superstitions are composed of "ideas" that cannot be traced back in this way.

2. In what sense is the idea of causation a fiction for Hume?
    The idea of a cause is the idea of one event making another happen, of a *necessary connection* between events. But we never observe such a connec-

101

tion; at best our experience can testify to *constant conjunctions* between events—that when an event of kind A happens, it is always accompanied by an event of kind B. Since real ideas must be traceable to impressions, and we have no impression of this connection, an important part of the idea of causation is fictional.

3.   What is Hume's view about the self or soul?

We do have the idea of a self—the idea of something simple and unchanging that persists through time and explains why we are the same today as we were years ago. Hume asks: From what impression is this idea derived? When he looks inside himself, he says, all he finds are various perceptions rapidly succeeding each other. So the idea of self or soul cannot be traced back to an impression. It is, in fact, a fiction, Hume thinks, created by confusing small changes with no changes at all, and similarity with sameness. We are but a bundle of perceptions.

4.   Explain how Hume thinks the necessity of actions (that they have causes) is compatible with the fact of liberty in actions (that we sometimes act freely).

Hume thinks we all believe that our actions have causes, and that their causes—our choices, wishes, desires—themselves have causes. For him, of course, this means merely that there are constant conjunctions of certain kinds of events. This is not incompatible with a certain kind of freedom or liberty, however; if we think of being free as being unconstrained, or unhindered in doing what we want to do, then we can be free even when caused—so long as we are able to do what we want. Freedom, understood this way, is not incompatible with causation but with constraint—a certain *kind* of causation that makes it impossible to satisfy our desires.

5.   Can God's existence be proved?

It cannot be proved by relying on relations of ideas, since these never entail any matter of fact. It cannot be proved a posteriori by relying on causality, because we never have experience of God's causing anything. Because it cannot be proved by relations of ideas and it cannot be proved by relying on matters of fact, it cannot be proved at all.

6.   How does Hume explain our judgment that a certain action is bad or wrong or vicious? In what do we find the viciousness of a vicious action?

There is nothing in the action itself that can explain it; in it no impression of a vicious quality can be found. The moral quality of the action lies, rather, in us—in our reaction to it. We feel a certain kind of disapproval informed by disinterested sympathy. We feel the action to be the opposite of agreeable or useful, either for ourselves or for others. Moral judgments are expressions of sentiment not conclusions of reason.

7.   What kind of skepticism does Hume approve of? And what kind does he not approve of?

He does not approve of "antecedent" skepticism, the sort that tries to doubt everything prior to any claims to know. He says we really can't do that; and if we could, there is no way we could then overcome it. Hume recommends a "mitigated" skepticism, however. This sort of skepticism will keep us from being dogmatic in our beliefs and superstitious in our behavior by helping us to keep in mind the strange infirmities of human understanding.

C. Essay Questions

1.   Compare Descartes and Hume on what can be known and how it can be known.

2.   In area after area, Hume is busy trying to convince us of the limitations of reason. Discuss how he goes about doing so with regard to causality, God, and morality.

3.   Compare Hobbes, Locke, Berkeley, and Hume on our knowledge of ourselves.

CHAPTER 16
IMMANUEL KANT
Rehabilitating Reason (Within Strict Limits)

ESSENTIAL POINTS

- The image of the dove and the necessity of resistance
- Needed: a critique of reason
- Kant's "Copernican Revolution"
- Critique
  * Kant's four questions
  * A transcendental investigation
- Judgments
  * The four possibilities; synthetic a priori as the key
  * Kant's four questions rephrased
- Geometry, Mathematics, Space, and Time
  * Universality and necessity as the two criteria for the a priori
  * Space and time as pure forms of intuition
  * Geometry and mathematics as constructions on the pure intuitions
- Common Sense, Science, and the A Priori Categories
  * Sensibility and understanding: their functions distinguished
  * A concept is a rule for operating on intuitions
  * Pure concepts or categories: a priori rules for structuring intuitions
  * Objectivity gained by the application of a category
  * Substance and causality as two crucial categories
  * No knowledge of things as they are in themselves
- Phenomena and Noumena
  * The emptiness of concepts without intuitions; the blindness of intuitions without concepts
  * The illusion of knowledge beyond possible experience
  * Kant's anatomy of the rational mind
- Reasoning and the Ideas of Metaphysics: God, World, and Soul
  * The structure of reasoning as the source of the Ideas of Pure Reason
  * The three directions taken by speculative metaphysics

- The Soul
  * The illusion of rational psychology
  * The "I" as a subject, not a possible object
- The World and the Free Will
  * Antinomies show that knowledge of the world in itself is not possible
  * The will is causally determined (phenomenally) yet may be free (noumenally)
- God
  * The inevitability of the concept of God
  * The emptiness of the concept of God
  * Critique of the ontological argument: existence is not a real predicate
  * Every judgment of existence is synthetic
- Reason and Morality
  * Looking for the supreme principle of morality
  * Nothing good without qualification but a good will
  * Will as an internal command of reason
  * Maxims express the subjective intention of an action
  * A good will must have a good maxim
  * The categorical imperative as the criterion for good maxims; its several forms
  * Autonomy: the rational legislation of every will for itself
  * The realm of ends: the world as it ought to be
  * Freedom as giving the law to oneself
  * Limiting knowledge to make room for faith

TEACHING SUGGESTIONS

1. Kant's image of the dove is so nice that it can be used again and again in teaching this chapter. It helps students grasp the point of many of Kant's more difficult ideas if they can see that he is showing us how the dove can fly, how it wants to fly where it cannot, and why it cannot fly out there.

2. Students have an intuitive grasp of golden rule fairness. In discussing Kant's ethical thought, it helps them understand universalization to pile example upon example showing where people are making exceptions for themselves from rules that they, at the same time, count on others observing.

EXAM QUESTIONS

A. Multiple-Choice Questions

1. The aim of Kant's critique of reason is
   - a. to demonstrate that reason can only be passion's slave.
   - x b. to reveal the a priori conditions of knowledge.
   - c. to show, contrary to Hume, that the scope of possible human knowledge is unlimited.
   - d. to show, contrary to Descartes, that human knowledge is not possible.

2. Synthetic a priori judgments, Kant tells us, are
   - a. knowable only in virtue of experience.
   - b. true by virtue of the fact that their denials are contradictory.
   - c. the only way of knowing things in themselves.
   - x d. a reflection of the structure of a rational mind.

3. The illusions of speculative metaphysics
   - x a. arise because of the very nature of reason itself.
   - b. pertain particularly to the realm of phenomena.
   - c. can be avoided by proving the existence of God.
   - d. have nothing to do with the nature of the self.

4. Concepts, according to Kant, are
   - a. faint copies of impressions.
   - b. one and all a priori.
   - x c. like rules for operating on some given material.
   - d. the only things guaranteeing knowledge of things in themselves.

5. The function of the categories is to
   - x a. construct an objective world.
   - b. illustrate how subjective all our opinions and beliefs really are.
   - c. serve as abstractions from sensible intuitions.
   - d. help the dove to fly in empty space.

6. According to Kant, knowledge of our own nature
   a. is impossible in any sense.
x b. is restricted to the way we appear in the realm of phenomena.
   c. is made possible by the category of substance, the application of which to ourselves demonstrates that we are essentially souls, not bodies.
   d. includes knowledge that we are free.

7. According to Kant, a good will is one that
   a. wills according to the dictates of one's society.
x b. wills to do its duty.
   c. obeys only hypothetical imperatives.
   d. is heteronomous.

8. The supreme principle of morality, Kant tells us,
   a. depends on the will of God.
   b. is different for each rational individual, because we are all autonomous choosers of the morally good.
   c. is universally accepted.
x d. forbids applying rules to others we don't apply to ourselves.

9. The categorical imperative
   a. is true in the same way that "Bachelors are unmarried" is true.
   b. tells us that if we want to be happy, we should respect the rights of others.
   c. bids us universalize all synthetic a priori principles.
x d. forbids manipulation of others for our own purposes.

10. Regarding freedom of the will, Kant says that
   a. we have no good reason to believe in it.
   b. though all our actions, noumenally conceived, have causes, yet we may be phenomenally free.
x c. morality would not be possible without it.
   d. we are free whenever we are not hindered in doing something we want to do.

11. I am autonomous in the realm of morality in the sense that
   x a. I am a legislator of the moral law for myself.
      b. my morality may not be the morality of others.
      c. what I want may not be what you want.
      d. I cannot be in error about what is right for me.

B. Short-Answer Questions

1. Kant says that a dove cannot fly in empty space; symbolically understood, this means:

A dove needs the resistance of the air in order to fly; just so, our thought needs the resistance of experience. Pure thought has often thought it could soar out beyond all possible experience and say what the world is like a priori. But that is an illusion. Our knowledge is confined to what we could possibly experience.

2. How are concepts like functions?

Concepts are like functions in that they are formal rules of procedure for operating on some content. Just as x^2 does not in itself designate any number but is a rule for producing some number given some value for x, so concepts are principles for operating on experiences: for categorizing, grouping, classifying, organizing, and relating experiences. Apart from some "filler," some intuition to structure, a concept is just an empty form.

3. Explain the idea of a synthetic a priori judgment, including both its semantic and its epistemological aspects. Why are these judgments puzzling?

Such a judgment is a priori (the epistemological side) in that it is knowable independently of experience. It is synthetic (the semantic side) in that its opposite is not a contradiction—that is, it is possibly true. What is puzzling is how we can know that just one of a pair of noncontradictory judgments must be true without consulting experience. Kant's whole philosophy, of course, rests on the claim that we are in possession of such judgments.

4. Explain the famous Kantian dictum: "Thoughts without content are empty, intuitions without concepts are blind."

Knowledge, Kant believes, is limited to what we could possibly experience. The reason is that the elements of thought—concepts—have no content in themselves; they are just functions for operating on a content in some way (structuring it, organizing it, classifying it...). Without some content supplied by sensibility, concepts have nothing to operate on and are empty forms. In contrast, if all we have is the sensory content of impressions, there is no knowledge either—just a booming, buzzing confusion. Intuitions (sensations, impressions) need the structuring of concepts to produce knowledge—indeed, even to produce the *experience* of an objective world!

5. Why, according to Kant, are we so sure that every event has a cause?

Because causality is one of the categories, an a priori concept or rule that structures our experience in time; without it we couldn't even recognize or identify particular events. It is a precondition of there being an objective world to experience at all.

6. In what way does Kant's claim that being is not a real predicate undercut the Ontological Argument—for instance, Descartes' third argument for God's existence?

To say, as Descartes does, that existence is a perfection is to suppose that it can play the same role as "knowledge" or "power." But if Kant is right, it is a concept of an altogether different sort. It does not enrich the conception of a possible being but says of that conception—whatever it is—that something actually corresponds to it. Since the argument depends on existence being a normal predicate, one of the argument's crucial premises is false.

7. If Descartes is rightly called a rationalist and Hume an empiricist, how would you describe Kant?

Kant incorporates aspects of both rationalism and empiricism. His critique is carried out by means of pure reason and reveals crucial elements of pure reason in all of knowledge. So Kant is in part a rationalist. But beyond possible experience there can be no knowledge, and that is a very empiricist line to take. Kant holds that a combination of reason and experience are the essential elements of human knowledge.

8. What is a maxim? What is the test for morally acceptable maxims?

A maxim is the subjective principle on which we act. Universalization is the test for moral acceptability. The question is: Could everyone act according to this maxim? Unless the answer is yes, the maxim is unacceptable and acting according to it would be immoral.

9. What is will, according to Kant? What is a good will? What makes a good will good?

Will is the last stage in rational deliberation, before action. It is expressed in an imperative addressed to oneself. A good will is one that acts out of respect for the moral law, one that does its duty. It is made good by the possibility of universalizing its maxim.

10. How does Kant use the distinction between things and persons in expressing the supreme principle of morality?

Things have only a relative value (relative to desires for them), which is called price. Persons have a kind of absolute value or dignity. The moral law forbids using persons as means only (for our own ends), which would be treating them as things. It demands that we respect them as persons.

11. Does Kant agree or disagree with Hume's dictum that reason is the slave of the passions? Explain.

He disagrees. Reason, particularly in its form of the categorical imperative, can criticize and rule over inclinations or passions. As rational creatures, we are capable of acting according to the rule of reason.

12. Kant says that he has found it necessary to deny knowledge to make room for faith. Knowledge of what? Faith in what?

Knowledge of certain things in themselves—for instance, in God, the soul, and freedom. He makes room for faith in these same things, though not arbitrarily, on the basis of practical reasons drawn from moral experience.

C. Essay Questions

1. How does Kant's "Copernican Revolution" address the problem of skepticism?

2. Kant says he was shaken by David Hume's analysis of causation. He calls it "Hume's problem." What was there about this analysis that awoke Kant from his "dogmatic slumber," and how does Kant think he has solved the problem?

3. Descartes, Hume, and Kant all have something to say about whether human beings can be free in their actions. Describe what it is in the new science that makes this a pressing question, and then sketch the line that each takes on human freedom.

4. What am I? Descartes, Hume, and Kant all discuss this question. Imagine that you are Immanuel Kant. Writing as you think he would write, discuss the views of Descartes and Hume on mind/self/soul, and express what you think is the truth about this matter.

5. You have borrowed $20 from an absent-minded friend. He has forgotten about it, and you are certain he will never remember. Moreover, your friend is well-off and will never miss it. To you, however, $20 means a lot.
   Describe what considerations a Kantian would—and would not—urge you to consider in deciding whether to repay the debt.

6. Explain how Kant thinks that morality, the laws of which are legislated by each person for himself or herself, can nevertheless be objective.

CHAPTER 17
GEORG WILHELM FRIEDRICH HEGEL
Taking History Seriously

ESSENTIAL POINTS

- Background
  - * Philosophers have generally not taken history seriously
  - * The lesson of the French Revolution: reason unfolds itself slowly in history
  - * Romantics against the Enlightenment
- Epistemology Internalized
  - * The circularity problem in previous epistemology
  - * Previous epistemology concedes too much to skepticism
  - * Phenomenology as the method by which to solve the problem of the criterion, reject skepticism, and avoid the circularity problem
  - * The key: development observed as progress
  - * We distinguish what is the case from what appears to be the case by comparisons internal to consciousness
  - * Beginning with sense certainty, we can observe consciousness as it zigzags its way to absolute knowledge
  - * What seems to be the most concrete, most certain knowledge, turns into its opposite
  - * Preserving what is true in sense certainty, consciousness develops into more adequate stages: perception, understanding, and self-consciousness
- Self and Others
  - * Desire is the first, inadequate, stage of self-consciousness.
  - * Recognition by another self-consciousness is required for one's own self-consciousness: how tortuous this process is
  - * The dialectic of master and slave
- Stoic and Skeptical Consciousness
  - * Stoic is free spirit, but abstract
  - * Skeptical freedom via suspension of judgment leads one to be a slave of custom

- Hegel's Analysis of Christianity
  * Spirit experiences itself as divided; projects its good side into the divine
  * The Mediator reconciles the divided self to itself
- Reason and Reality: The Theory of Idealism
  * The substance of the world is a subject, is reason itself, but implicitly, not yet in actuality
  * Absolute Knowledge as the World Spirit's knowing that it is all of reality—subject and object both
- Spirit Made Objective: The Social Character of Ethics
  * Culture as the manifestation of reason in history
    — Custom first, the immediate stage
    — Then morality
    — Then the rational society of free individuals
  * Critique of Kant's ethics as unduly abstract
- History and Freedom
  * Freedom is the goal history is moving toward
  * The negativity in this process and the cunning of reason
  * The state as the "idea" manifest on earth
  * The owl of Minerva

TEACHING SUGGESTIONS

When teaching Hegel, I cover the board with diagrams, drawn as we go along, of the progress of consciousness as Hegel understands it. The negativities are stressed, together with the dialectical urges to move to something more satisfactory. Doing it in this dynamic way—in class—is better, I think, than giving them a diagram already worked out ahead of time to study. More Hegelian, too. (You could do it with an overhead projector, too, revealing new stages as appropriate.)

EXAM QUESTIONS
A. Multiple-Choice Questions

1. Hegel says that the "problem of the criterion" cannot be solved by the philosopher,
    - x a. but that's all right, since it is in the process of solving itself.
    - b. so we have to resign ourselves to living without knowledge.
    - c. because we are caught in a circle that cannot be got out of.
    - d. and it's a good thing, too, since that makes room for progress and development.

2. Phenomenology, as practiced by Hegel, is
    - a. a method of getting beyond mere phenomena to absolute reality.
    - b. a way of validating the phenomena experienced by the arbitrary individual.
    - x c. a technique of observing consciousness develop.
    - d. irrelevant to reality but significantly relevant to phenomena.

3. At the stage of sense-certainty, consciousness
    - a. has absolute knowledge of its contents.
    - x b. is wholly receptive and immediate.
    - c. is certain that it derives from the senses—eyes, ears, and so on.
    - d. can say with absolute certainty what is being experienced through the senses.

4. The dialectic of master and slave
    - a. demonstrates the exploitation of slaves throughout history and condemns it.
    - b. shows how we are all slaves, even though some of us take ourselves to be masters.
    - c. constitutes a practical prescription for freeing slaves, no matter what stage of history they may be in.
    - x d. describes a necessary stage in the progress toward self-consciousness.

5. Christianity, according to Hegel,
   - x a. is the genuine expression of one essential stage in the development of consciousness.
   - b. expresses an unhappy consciousness about which the best that can be done is to accept it.
   - c. is correct at least in this, that it sees a clear distinction between God and the soul.
   - d. is the stage toward which Absolute Spirit is tending.

6. Hegel's philosophy is aptly characterized as Absolute Idealism because
   - a. the Absolute Spirit is an idealistic dreamer of dreams that could never be realized.
   - x b. whatever is real has its reality only in relation to the Absolute.
   - c. without ideals, we are absolutely lost.
   - d. reality is constituted in the consciousness of each absolutely unique individual.

7. In the stages of objective spirit, consciousness
   - a. objectifies itself in the world of nature.
   - b. understands itself as just one object in the natural world along with others.
   - c. moves from Stoic to Skeptical to Christian consciousness.
   - x d. develops toward a rational society.

8. In Hegel's view,
   - a. individuals join together in a "contract" to create the state.
   - x b. individuals are related to the state as the liver is to the body it serves.
   - c. because individual human beings are metaphysically prior to any community, the state is only a fiction.
   - d. history is tending toward a state that will be a "slaughter house."

9. The goal of historical development, according to Hegel, is
    a. unknowable.
    b. absurd.
    x c. freedom.
    e. insufficient to justify the horrors of history.

10. The owl of Minerva, Hegel tells us, spreads its wings only at dusk. This means that
    a. owls can see better at night than in the daytime.
    b. Hegel believes in the old Greek gods.
    c. philosophers are the only ones wise enough to give instruction as to what the world ought to be.
    x d. the world can be understood only retrospectively.

B. Short-Answer Questions

1. How does Hegel propose to solve the problem of finding a criterion for knowledge?

Hegel does not himself propose to solve it, arguing that to solve the problem of the criterion we would have to know something before we could be sure we knew anything—and that is incoherent. Fortunately, the problem is in the process of being solved by the dialectical process of consciousness and its objects mutually adjusting to each other. Consciousness is moving toward an identity of subject and object, in which it will know that its objects are nothing outside itself, since they are constituted out of its own resources. That end point will be "absolute knowledge," and the problem of the criterion will have been solved.

2. Why does consciousness in the state of sense-certainty need to move beyond it?

Because it recognizes its own inadequacy. Consciousness by nature desires to know, to make the object its own. But in sense-certainty the lack of a rich conceptual apparatus for expressing the nature of the "object" leaves the object alien. With its own resources, it can manage only a very inadequate grasp of the subject matter in terms of the bare concepts, "here," "now," "I", etc. The inadequacy of these notions to grasp the object force the next stage.

3. Why is conflict involved in the development of self-consciousness?

Desire, the first stage of self-consciousness, is the clear recognition of something as other than I am, together with the project bringing it back within the sphere of my control. When the other is another self-consciousness, what I want is for the other to recognize me as a self-conscious being; but I also want to control that recognition. The other naturally resists that control but has a parallel desire with respect to myself. Hence, conflict.

4. Why is it the slave, rather than the master, who moves Spirit forward toward self-consciousness?

The slave has a (partial) image of independence in the master but, more important, can come to recognize herself in her work, an objectification of her capacities and talents, which functions as a kind of mirror to reveal the slave to herself. The master cannot consider the recognition that comes from the slave as worth much, since it comes after all from a slave he controls.

5. How does the Unhappy Consciousness move beyond Stoic and Skeptical consciousness. And what makes it unhappy?

Stoics and Skeptics identify themselves with the *consciousness* of objects—consciousness of the body, consciousness of the results of one's actions, consciousness of all the worldly facts making up one's worldly nature. All these objects are other than oneself, distinct, different, alien, arbitrary, accidental. But the Unhappy Consciousness recovers these alien objects, recognizing that they too are part of oneself. It suffers from the contradiction within the self—good and evil, rational and arbitrary, free and determined. Hence it is unhappy.

6. Why is Hegelian reason able to succeed in its aims, while Kantian reason cannot?

Kant sees reason as a drive for completeness, for grasping the unconditioned. But that is to go beyond possible experience, which we cannot do. Hegel's reason, on the other hand, sees that there cannot be any object that is completely and forever alien to itself. There is not, could not be, an object that was not an object for it. So all reality is relative to consciousness; and when consciousness becomes aware of that, it realizes that it is not limited (as Kant thought), and there is no need to make room for faith.

7. Sketch the development of society from the stage of Custom, through that of Morality, to Ethics.

In the stage of Custom, individuals do not experience their culture as alien from themselves but are at one with it. Morality is the Socratic-Kantian stage in which individuals set themselves over against their culture, ask it embarrassing questions about justification, and legislate the Moral Law for themselves. In Ethics, the gap is closed once more, this time not because individuals seamlessly identify themselves with whatever the culture happens to be, but because the culture conforms to the rational moral requirements of individuals—who now find in the laws and customs a reflection of their own rationality and freedom.

8.   What justifies the horrors of history, according to Hegel?
The end toward which history is driving: absolute knowledge, freedom, and reason. It is only because all this slaughter and misery must necessarily be passed through as negative stages to get to this glorious goal that history has any justification.

9.   What is phenomenology?
Phenomenology is the discipline of carefully observing the phenomena —in this case, the phenomena of consciousness itself. So phenomenology does not argue or explain; it describes. Hegel uses it to describe the dialectical development of consciousness from inadequate to more and more adequate comprehension of its objects.

10.   Explain Hegel's Absolute Idealism as the theory of how reason and reality are related?
There is no object without a subject. The subject to which reality corresponds is not the individual, of course, nor a culture at a given time, but the World Spirit, which is developing according to necessary dialectical patterns. At each stage, reality is partly rational in an explicit way; but it is never completely or concretely rational. Still the rational is the real and whatever is real is at least implicitly and potentially rational. The rationality implicit in any stage of development will become explicit in the goal toward which history is moving—the absolute knowledge of the World Spirit, where explicit reason will govern all things.

11.   How does Hegel think of God? How is God related to the world? To us?
God = The World Spirit = the Absolute = Reason = Reality. God is not the creator of the world but its substance. In himself God is implicitly all of reality; history is making what is implicit explicit and concrete. So in time God is coming to self-consciousness, and we are the "location" where this process is occurring. We are God in the process of moving toward the goals of absolute knowledge and freedom.

C. Essay Questions

1. Compare what Hegel has to say about freedom and the arbitrary will with Hume's compatibilist analysis of human liberty.

2. Descartes worried about skepticism concerning the "external" world and thought he had found a criterion for knowledge in the clarity and distinctness of certain ideas. Imagine that you are Hegel. What do you say to Descartes? Begin your answer with these words: "Look, René, . . ."

3. What does Hegel appreciate about Kant's theory of morality? And how does he criticize it?

4. How is Hegel's view concerning the state connected to his views about freedom and history?

5. How, according to Hegel, are reason and reality related? Contrast his view to that of Kant.

CHAPTER 18
KIERKEGAARD AND MARX
Two Ways to "Correct" Hegel

ESSENTIAL POINTS

- Kierkegaard: On Individual Existence
    * The pseudonymous authors present distinct modes of life as possibilities for choice
    * The Aesthetic
        — Aim: to keep life interesting, to avoid boredom
        — Two poles: immediacy (Don Juan) and reflection (the Seducer)
        — Rules for an interesting life; the key is to stay in control
    * The Ethical
        — Critique of the aesthetic: you can't be a self that way
        — Falling in love vs. the engagement of the will in a marriage
        — The judge as the defender of romantic love
        — Serious choice brings with it ethical categories—and continuity in the self
        — The crucial choice: aesthetic or ethical
    * The Religious
        — The knights of infinite resignation and of faith
        — Varieties of failure in the task of being willing to be the self that we are: despair, which is sin
        — Faith is a passion, not a kind of sub-par understanding; Hegel is mistaken in thinking philosophy can go farther
    * The Individual
        — There cannot be an existential system
        — What sort of relation to the truth is possible for an existing individual
        — The task: to become oneself; we live by a leap
- Marx: Beyond Alienation and Exploitation
    * What Marx learned from Hegel
    * Bringing Hegel back to earth
    * Alienation, Exploitation, and Private Property
        — The struggle between capital and labor

- The worker as a commodity
- Workers alienated from their work, from themselves, from the products of their labor, and from fellow workers
- Greed and the money system
* Communism
    - Class struggles now sharpen and intensify; revolution
    - The goal: freedom beyond alienation and exploitation

TEACHING SUGGESTIONS

1. In teaching Kierkegaard, I have always felt that personal stories bring his points to life. I demonstrate to the class that I am growing bald. That is part of my immediacy—just a fact about me. But, I say, I cannot just *be* bald. I am also reflectively aware of being bald. So I have to take up some attitude toward it, make some choices. Shall I be ashamed of it? Try to hide it? Shall I get a hair piece or have implants? Or shall I flaunt it—maybe shave it all off? Make a joke of it? And so on.

Well, you can make up your own examples—maybe about falling in love and having to do something about that. Whatever. This sort of thing makes Don Juan and the Seducer and the Judge come alive—and also the discussion of despair and its opposite, faith.

2. Now that Communism seems nearly dead, interest in Marx can be sharpened by asking: What remains of value there?

EXAM QUESTIONS
A. Multiple-Choice Questions

KIERKEGAARD
1. Kierkegaard's young man, A, searching for a way to keep life interesting, advises that you
   x a. learn the art of remembering and forgetting.
      b. find an interesting wife or husband.
      c. try to imitate the life of Don Juan, who certainly had an interesting time of it.
      d. travel to exotic places.

2. Judge William's either/or, he tells us, represents
   x a. choosing or not (really, seriously, passionately) choosing.
       b. a choice between good and evil lives.
       c. the choice between living ethically or living religiously.
       d. the fact that whatever you choose, you will regret it.

3. The life of faith, Kierkegaard and his pseudonyms tell us,
       a. is the most otherworldly life imaginable.
       b. is a stage we go through on the way toward rational understanding.
   x c. is a life of the greatest passion, the most intense inwardness.
       d. is the life lived by the knight of infinite resignation who resigns (lets go of) everything earthly.

4. Despair
       a. occurs when something goes badly wrong in life.
   x b. can manifest itself as being willing, defiantly, to be oneself.
       c. is the opposite of virtue.
       d. can be dispelled by chanting the mantra: "I'm OK, I'm OK, . . ."

5. With respect to the notion of a "system," Kierkegaard's pseudonym Johannes Climacus says:
       a. Have a system, or do not have a system, you will regret both.
       b. A logical system is impossible.
       c. A system can develop internally through time, as Hegel clearly showed us.
   x d. Since a system of reality is not possible for us, the highest truth available for us is an objective uncertainty held fast in passionate inwardness.

MARX

1. Marx agrees with Hegel that
   a. history is fundamentally the story of the development of consciousness.
   b. it is not enough to understand the world; philosophers should seek to change it.
   x c. antagonism and opposition have characterized history to this day.
   d. the evils of history have no resolution and must simply be born with resignation.

2. Private property, according to Marx,
   a. develops as a natural right in the state of nature.
   b. will be protected in a good state more securely than it now is.
   c. will be multiplied and shared by all when machines replace workers on the assembly lines.
   x d. is the product of alienated labor.

3. Marx holds that class struggle
   x a. will cease after a workers' revolution in which they seize control of the means of production.
   b. cannot ever be wholly eliminated because of the greed of human beings.
   c. is gradually diminishing in the wake of the explosion of goods available to all.
   d. is fundamentally a matter of class envy.

B. Short-Answer Questions

KIERKEGAARD

1. Under what categories does an aesthete organize his or her life? Describe two ways this might work out, using the examples of Don Juan and the Seducer.

An aesthete lives under the categories "interesting" and "boring." The idea is to maximize the interesting, and to this end, one must ensure that one is always in control. Don Juan lives an interesting life in the *immediate*. He is quite unreflective, virtually a force of nature, simply wanting a woman and taking her. But Don Juan can exist only in art—as in Mozart's *Don Giovanni*. The Seducer is at the opposite extreme, *reflective* to a fault, always scheming, arranging, organizing, manipulating, so that his life has that aesthetic edge he prizes.

2. What advice would Kierkegaard's young aesthete, A, give you about how to live your life?

Keep life interesting; avoid boredom. To do that you have to create your own life as a work of art you can enjoy. And that requires control. So—avoid commitments—friends, a spouse, business. Live for the moment, for only in the moment does enjoyment exist.

3. Judge William, writing to A, speaks of his either/or. What is that? And how does it mark the difference between A's form of life and the Judge's?

The Judge advises A that he cannot succeed in his project and urges decision, choice, commitment. A passionate, wholehearted choice will catapult A right into another sphere of existence—the ethical, in which good and evil become the significant categories. The principal either/or, however, is not that between good and evil. It is between the style of life in which good and evil are meaningful and the style of life in which they are not—between the aesthetic (the amoral) and the ethical.

4. What is the Judge's view of the relation between romantic love and marriage?

Romantic love is something immediate. One falls into it—and out of it. Its watchword is "To see her is to love her." Yet, as love, it has in it the impression of eternity; the lovers believe their love will last. So long as it remains merely immediate (just nature), however, it won't in fact last, and that leads to cynicism about love. But the Judge is the friend of romantic love. He says that if one brings the will and duty and commitment to love, it can fulfill its promise. The way this is done is in marriage, where the partners pledge, promise, to keep their love alive.

5. What is despair? What is the condition of a self when despair is completely eradicated?

Despair is not being willing to be oneself; that is the formula for sin. Despair manifests itself in doublemindedness—in rationalization, self-deception, insincerity, hypocrisy, etc. When despair is eradicated one is willing to be oneself; this is the formula for faith. But since one is constantly failing to be oneself—is in a state of sin—being willing to be oneself involves faith in forgiveness and in the "power that posited the self."

6. What is characteristic of a system? What would an existential system be? And how does Kierkegaard attack this notion?

The mark of a system is finality; nothing can be added to it. All true propositions are already embedded in its basic assumptions. An existential system would be an account of all of reality—such as Hegel promised. In such a system, all the true propositions about reality would find a home, related to each other in such a way that none could be different without changing the whole. Kierkegaard asks: Who is to write such a system? Surely an existing individual. But an existing individual is not yet finished, facing choices not yet made. So there is no way any system about reality could be written by an existing individual.

MARX

1. What does Marx mean when he says that "life is not determined by consciousness, but consciousness by life"?

Unlike Hegel, who thinks that spirit, consciousness, and the quest for knowledge are the moving forces in reality, Marx believes that material reality is fundamental. Before we can think, we must eat; and to eat we must organize modes of production for the things we need. Ideas, theories, views—whether philosophical, religious, or political—are merely reflections of the fundamental material realities. They are ideologies that have no independent status.

2. What is the origin of private property, according to Marx?

Private property originates in alienated labor, Marx says. The worker labors and produces value, but it is value in the hands of another—the capitalist. The worker has virtually no property; private property is the property of the owners of the means of production.

3. Describe some forms of worker alienation.

Workers are alienated from their work; they cannot express their humanity in it, their creativity. In their work they are no more than machines, or animals. They are alienated from the products of their labor; it belongs to another. They are alienated from each other by the competition for jobs. And they are alienated from their employers who are exploiting them.

4. According to Marx, what would a communist revolution accomplish?

It would bring about the abolition of the private property that has been accumulated by exploiting the workers. Political power would wither away, together with class divisions. Those who do the work would control the means of production. And people would live free and rich lives, the development of each being the condition for the development of all.

C. Essay Questions

1. In what different ways can Kierkegaard and Marx be seen as reacting critically to Hegelian philosophy?
    (a) What was there about Hegelianism that each objected to?
    (b) What forms did their alternatives to Hegelianism take?

2. Kierkegaard admires Socrates extravagantly. In what ways is his indirect communication like the conversations Socrates held with his fellow Athenians?

CHAPTER 19
THE UTILITARIANS
Moral Rules and the Happiness of All (Including Women)

ESSENTIAL POINTS

- The Classic Utilitarians
    * Happiness as pleasure and the absence of pain
    * Psychological and ethical hedonism
    * Not the agent's happiness, but the greatest happiness altogether is the standard
    * Impartiality: each one to count for one
    * Bentham's utility calculus
    * Mill and the quality of pleasure: how to judge
    * Consequentialism
    * Proof of the utilitarian principle
    * Replies to objections
        — Does not aim too low, as the pleasures of a human being are different from the pleasures of a pig
        — If unrealizable, at least minimize unhappiness and don't exaggerate what happiness is
        — Allows for self-sacrifice
        — Does not demand perfection in motives
        — Allows for admiration of character
        — Not ungodly
        — Not impractical, as secondary principles may be learned
    * Justice and rights are founded in the need for security
- The Rights of Women
    * The state of English law regarding women
    * Why this situation has perpetuated itself
    * Rousseau on the education of women; its bad effects
    * Needed: equality before the law, independence, and mutual respect
    * Virtue to be founded in human nature, not in sex

TEACHING SUGGESTIONS

1. A contrast between utilitarian consequentialism and the Kantian "There are some things you just don't do, no matter

what the consequences" is always gripping. Matters of justice or fairness raise the issues most clearly. Examples are a necessity, and can be used to display the subtleties in both positions.

2. Many current issues can be raised in connection with the question of women's rights. How far we have come is striking. What remains to be done?

EXAM QUESTIONS
A. Multiple-Choice Questions

1. An ethical hedonist will
   a. favor the pleasures of others over his or her own.
   b. think that we all, always, pursue pleasure over anything else.
   c. disdain pleasure in favor of ethical correctness.
   x d. count the pleasures of all as equally important.

2. Bentham's calculus of utility
   x a. was designed to help legislators write good laws.
   b. relies on Newton's calculus for its structure.
   c. regards the intensity of a pain as more important than the duration of a pleasure.
   d. includes considerations of the quality of pleasures, as determined by the majority of those who have experienced them.

3. The basic idea of consequentialism is that
   a. all consequences of a given act are equally important in trying to decide whether to do that act.
   x b. we should look to the consequences when judging the moral rightness of an act.
   c. we all have our own ideas about the consequences of our acts, so morality will be different for everyone.
   d. happiness doesn't count as much as consequences.

4. In replying to objections that have been raised to utilitarianism, Mill states that
    a. it is better to be a fool satisfied than a Socrates dissatisfied, for the fool experiences the most pleasure.
    b. happiness for all is a good goal, as striving for it is the way to get the most happiness for yourself.
x c. it is not impractical, because we don't need to calculate the consequences of every act at the time of doing it.
    d. everything should be done from the motive of happiness for all.

5. Regarding justice, Mill says that
x a. rules of justice have particular importance because they deal with something very important to us: our security.
    b. it is always possible that the consequences of an act can be so beneficial that they will outweigh considerations of justice.
    c. justice is of such a pleasurable quality as to outweigh any quantitative considerations about pleasure.
    d. justice is godly, and so utilitarianism is not opposed to it.

6. Wollstonecraft thinks that women in her day
    a. deserve what they have gotten.
x b. have deliberately been treated in such a way as to make them weak, meddlesome, and cunning.
    c. are superior to men in virtue.
    d. should engage in armed rebellion, if necessary, to attain their rights.

B. Short-Answer Questions

1. Explain the principle of utility. What makes this a moral principle—rather than just a piece of prudential or self-interested advice?

    Act so as to bring about by your action the set of consequences that produces the most happiness overall. It is moral in that it treats everyone alike—impartially. You are to consider your alternatives, weigh the consequences relevant to happiness, and choose to do the action that has the greatest balance of happiness over unhappiness—for everyone concerned.

2. How does Mill defend utilitarianism against the charge that to take pleasure as a standard for morality is to espouse a morality for pigs.

"Better a Socrates unsatisfied than a pig satisfied," says Mill. Human beings have more sophisticated pleasures than pigs, so the pleasure standard will specify different behavior for humans than for pigs. It is a misunderstanding of utilitarianism to think of it as a "piggish" morality.

3. How does Mill defend utilitarianism against the charge that it makes it impossible to understand admiration for people who act in a self-sacrificial way.

What is the point of self-sacrifice, Mill asks? He holds that unless it is for the sake of increasing the general happiness, it is not admirable. But if it does increase the general happiness, that sort of self-sacrifice is right in line with the principle of utility.

4. How does Mill defend utilitarianism against the charge that the general happiness is too high a standard?

We can approximate it, even if we cannot wholly achieve it. Moreover, we can do a lot to minimize pain and unhappiness, and that is also part of the utilitarian rule.

5. What problem is justice thought to raise for the Utilitarians? How does Mill argue that there is, in the last analysis, no conflict between justice and utility?

It looks like one might, in certain circumstances, actually increase the general happiness by doing something unjust—for instance, by executing an innocent person. Mill claims that justice is connected with rights, and rights with the fundamental condition for happiness—security of person and property. So a utilitarian seeking happiness will not undermine the general security by doing unjust acts. In short, Mill believes it will never pay—in terms of happiness—to be unjust.

6. What general features of an action determine whether it is morally right or wrong? Contrast this utilitarian view with Kant's account of what makes actions right or wrong.

The consequences—particularly those consequences that have to do with the pleasure and pain produced—determine rightness and wrongness. The aim is to do the act—for whatever reason—that in fact produces the greatest amount of happiness overall. This contrasts with Kant's view that what counts, morally speaking, is the intention with which an action is performed; only those actions that originate in a good will—actions done out of respect for the moral law —are morally praiseworthy.

7.   What bad consequences do Wollstonecraft and Mill see flowing from the differential treatment of women?

It seems that there is a different moral standard for women. They are praised for being pleasing to men, and that is corrupting. It concentrates their attention on appearances, on trivialities, and leads them to cunning subtleties in an attempt to seize as much control as they can. Their lack of education keeps them ignorant of larger matters, which they still cannot help but meddle in. And it deprives humanity of a great deal of talent, energy, and good influence that women can contribute. Finally, it perpetuates injustice.

C. Essay Questions

1.   Compare Kantian ethics with the ethics of utilitarianism, pointing out both similarities and differences.

2.   Would a Kantian or a utilitarian be the best friend of women's rights? Explain your answer in some detail.

CHAPTER 20
FRIEDRICH NIETZSCHE
The Value of Existence

ESSENTIAL POINTS

- Pessimism and Tragedy
  * The wisdom of Silenus sets the problem: how to live in the face of the horrors of existence
  * Apollo the god of reason, of moderation, of the epic
  * Dionysus the god of excess, of intoxication, of the lyric
  * Schopenhauer: the world as will and representation
  * Music expresses the primal oneness of the will
  * The key role of the (Dionysian) chorus of satyrs, who in their chants dream the (Apollinian) drama on the stage
  * How tragedy redeems: identification with the eternal life of the will
  * Only the aesthetic quality of our lives can make them worth living
- Good-bye True World
  * Traditional metaphysics is confession, not description of reality
  * The errors of philosophy are grounded in language, needs, and wishes
  * Nature is valueless, and there is no true reality behind it
  * How the true world became a fable: the stages
  * Why Nietzsche needs to rethink the problem of the value of existence: he can no longer rely on the "true world" of Schopenhauerian will
- The Death of God
  * What it means that God is dead
  * The ways gods die
  * The death of God poses the problem of nihilism
- Revaluation of Values
  * We need to determine the weights of things anew because present weights took God and true worlds for granted
  * Many moralities
  * Master Morality/Slave Morality

- The morality of the masters founded in their judgment that they are the "good"; "bad" as the shadow of this judgment; a life-affirming morality
- The morality of the slaves founded in resentment, a "No!" to "evil"—that is, to the good of the masters; "good" as the shadow, designating their own weakness
- Slave morality is our morality: the demand for equal rights
- The self-deceptions of slave morality
- The Overman
  * The overman as the meaning of the earth
    - Remains faithful to the earth
    - Possesses the great health
    - Creates himself and creates values in creating himself
    - Overcomes himself, gives style to his life, lives aesthetically
    - Loves himself and, in loving himself, despises all that is yet weak and unmastered in himself
    - Praises the friend, not the neighbor
    - Recognizes that life is essentially will to power
    - Is aware of the order of rank among men
    - Affirms eternal recurrence, the ultimate yes-saying
  * Dionysus absorbs Apollo, is identified with life, with will to power, affirmation, joy, laughter

TEACHING SUGGESTIONS

It is easy for students to get carried along by Nietzsche's passionate prose, especially because many of them have views rather like some of his to begin with. I encourage that. Then, after they have drunk deeply from the Nietzschean cup, it is time for some hard questions. For example: (a) Is Nietzsche fair to Christianity? Does he understand it or misunderstand it (reference Augustine, Aquinas, Kierkegaard)? (b) Do we really want to give up equality as a goal? (c) Is it true that our best values are the result of resentment and revenge, a consequence of lies and hypocrisy? (d) Is God dead? (e) Does aesthetics always trump morality? And so on. An excellent stimulus to thought.

EXAM QUESTIONS
A. Multiple-Choice Questions

1. Nietzsche looks to Greek tragedy
   a. for a portrayal of how to live morally in an indifferent universe.
   b. to teach us what pessimism really means.
   x c. for a solution to the problem of the value of existence.
   d. where Apollo is shown to conquer Dionysus, to the benefit of all.

2. In his early book, *The Birth of Tragedy*, Nietzsche relies on Schopenhauer for
   a. an understanding of how to quiet the will and get relief from the suffering of desire.
   x b. the concept of a primal oneness underlying the phenomenal world of individuals.
   c. the principle of individuation, which makes individuals into the ultimate realities.
   d. his music dramas, which Nietzsche thought indicated a rebirth of tragedy in the modern world.

3. Nietzsche believes the problem of the value of existence can be solved only
   x a. by making our lives into works of art.
   b. by recognizing the values inherent in things as they are placed on the Great Chain of Being.
   c. by living according to a strict moral code.
   d. by belief in a loving God.

4. When true worlds become fables,
   a. we need to invent new ones.
   b. we are left with only the apparent world.
   c. there has been a failure of reason, and we need to try to be more rational.
   x d. we have reached the high point of humanity.

5. What does it mean that God is dead?
    a. It is obvious to all that there is no God.
    x b. Nihilism threatens.
    c. We need to invent new gods.
    d. Christ died on the cross for our sins.

6. A revaluation of values
    a. would ask the question: What values does true morality endorse?
    b. cannot be accomplished because it would involve you in a circle, assuming some values to judge others.
    x c. is needed because of the death of God.
    d. would criticize present values as degenerate and try to bring us back to the values of our ancestors.

7. The main difference between master morality and slave morality is that
    a. the masters think of the slaves as evil.
    b. the slaves think of the masters as bad.
    x c. one morality is founded in affirmation and the other in resentment.
    d. only master morality, the morality of the powerful, has survived to the present day.

8. An overman, as Nietzsche portrays him,
    x a. remains faithful to the earth.
    b. overcomes selfishness in himself and fosters equality.
    c. must kill God over and over.
    d. agrees with the soothsayer that all is the same and nothing is worthwhile.

9. An overman, as Nietzsche portrays him,
    a. is a rope, a rope over an abyss.
    b. is first a child, then a camel, then a lion.
    c. creates himself first and then makes all his disciples into overmen, too.
    x d. is the poet of his life.

10. An overman, as Nietzsche portrays him,
    a. is possessed of a deep seriousness about life that makes it all worthwhile.
  x b. is the meaning of the earth.
    c. is a master of taking revenge on those who try to belittle him.
    d. pities those not fortunate enough to be blessed with the health and strength to be overmen, too.

11. Affirming eternal recurrence
    a. serves as a test of your intelligence; only those bright enough to understand it can become overmen.
    b. causes nausea in overmen.
    c. is what the small man does, the man of little brain and no virtue.
  x d. is a sign that you are well-disposed toward your life.

B. Short-Answer Questions

1. What kind of solution to the problem of "the value of existence" does Nietzsche envisage?

An aesthetic solution. Only through aesthetics can the world and human life be justified—by seeing them as works of art. Art has value, even when—as in tragedy—it portrays the terrible and bloody end of individuals. If we could but come to see our own lives in analogy with the lives of the tragic heroes, our lives would have value and meaning. That is the proper way to overcome pessimism.

2. How does Nietzsche use the metaphysics of Schopenhauer to explain the "metaphysical comfort" that tragedy supplies?

Schopenhauer agrees with Kant that the world as we experience it is merely a phenomenon—the way things appear to us. This world is, as he puts it, idea or representation. It is the expression, however, of reality itself that has the character of will—surging, yearning, desiring, pressing always into existence. In tragedy the audience, identifying with the Dionysian chorus, views the illusory dream of individuals presented on the stage—who despite their best efforts end in destruction. It redeems by showing us that individuality—our own included—is not ultimate reality, but merely a dream. In reality we are identical with life itself, with the will, which is neither individuated nor mortal. So tragedy "saves" by showing us our true nature in such a way that we are consoled.

3. Why does Nietzsche think "true worlds" have become a fable? What replaces them?

Metaphysics has shown itself to be a set of projections by the philosophers, not a dispassionate description of the truth of things. Philosophers need the world to be so-and-so, they exercise their will to power, and they produce a world that is so-and-so. Honesty has also led us to see that language betrays us into thinking that reality mirrors its peculiarities. And human needs have fostered errors. When true worlds fade, however, it is not the apparent world that is left. That would make no sense, as "appearance" lives off of its contrast with "reality." What is left is just *the world.*

4. What does it mean that God is dead? And what danger threatens after God's death?

It means that people no longer believe in God, though they may not have realized that yet. When God dies, the center of our world vanishes, the anchor for our values, the judge of right and wrong. The threat is nihilism, where everything seems flat and alike and nothing is worthwhile. Life seems meaningless.

5. What would be an overman's reaction to learning of the death of God?

An Overman would affirm the Death of God. If there were gods, how could he bear not to be a god as well? The Death of God correlates with the overman remaining faithful to the earth and to the body, to his opposition to all afterworlds, and to striving for a meaning for the earth. Previously humans had looked for the guarantee of value and meaning beyond the earth; now it must be sought here. The Death of God opens pathways to new values and the creation of oneself—no longer limited by rules from on high.

6. Describe master morality.

Master morality arose, according to Nietzsche, among the strong, the powerful, the noble, the rulers. They, possessed of a vibrant health and physicality, pronounced their lives good. In other words, they affirmed their own lives, said yes to what they were. What was other than they—low, weak, sickly, lying, dirty, vulgar—they pronounced bad. But the bad was simply the shadow of the glory that was they.

7. Describe slave morality.

The slaves suffered from the oppression of their masters—and they resented it. But they couldn't do anything about it because they were too weak. So that resentment festered and grew. What oppressed them they called evil, a concept born of the desire for revenge and no-saying. This was their original value-creation. Themselves they called good—the meek, the humble, the patient, the serving—baptizing all that they could not help being into virtues, a work of self-deception.

8. What would be an overman's relation to will to power?

The overman affirms the will to power as the essence of all life. All life wants to be master—of its situation and of itself. So life is essentially overcoming, particularly self-overcoming. The overman is the one in whom will to power is at a maximum, the one who has given style to his life, the artist whose greatest work is himself. Wherever the overman looks, he sees the will to power at work. The will to truth, the creative will, the will to create values—all manifestations of the will to power. Indeed, even the resentment and revenge of the powerless is will to power—the will to power of the weak.

9. What does Zarathustra say about friends and neighbors?

Not the neighbor, I teach you, says Zarathustra, but the friend. He will speak to companions, to friends, not to the mob. He suspects that we flee from ourselves in crowding around the neighbor, that our love of the neighbor is just our dissatisfaction with ourselves. An overman will love his friends as he loves himself—with hardness, demanding much from them, and with no pity.

10. What does Zarathustra say about equality?

Men are not equal, Zarathustra says, and an overman would agree. The doctrine of equality is revenge, spiteful poison, spread through the tarantula's bite. It is a doctrine of weakness that would pull the strong down to their own level, that says, "No one *shall* be better, greater, stronger; we'll see to it!" What would life be worth if there were nothing to inspire, nothing to generate awe and even fear—if all were at the level of the herd, the superfluous, the all-to-many? Man, as Zarathustra says, is something that should be overcome!

11. What is an overman's opinion of selfishness?

The overman loves himself, and in loving himself despises all that is not yet perfect in himself. He climbs up and over himself toward himself. Loving himself he will not be distracted from the task of self-perfection—not even by pity for others. The selfishness of the overman is beyond cowardice, subservience, self-pity, patience, and humility. There is another selfishness that Zarathustra (and the overman) do not admire—the selfishness of the weak and degenerate, who desperately grasp at any advantage and are willing to do *anything* to get it.

12. How does an overman react to news of eternal recurrence?

An overman accepts eternal recurrence, and in so doing signals "how well disposed" to himself he is. Understanding that everything is connected and that you can't have just the "good" parts, the question eternal recurrence poses is this: Given that, would you wish to have it all again—and again, and again? An overman is strong enough, healthy enough, satisfied enough with himself to say yes.

13. What is Zarathustra's reaction to nihilism?

Nihilism is the threat posed by the Death of God. If hitherto mankind had hitched its meaning for life to God, what happens when God dies? It looks like the death of meaning—as if the soothsayer is right, that all is empty, flat, all the same. Nothing seems worthwhile, because the facts in the world contain no value and the value-giver has died. This is the modern equivalent of Greek pessimism. Zarathustra considers it the ultimate challenge and finds an answer to it in the overman, who *shall* be the meaning of the earth.

14. What do Zarathustra and the overman say about pity?

Pity is, according to Zarathustra, a negative emotion, a denial of life. The overman will be beyond all pity—certainly beyond self-pity. Christianity (as Nietzsche understands it) is a religion of pity. It was pity (among other things) that finally did in God himself—he was so filled with pity for man that his own life simply withered away and died. The overman will be a bed for his friend when the friend suffers—but a hard bed, a field cot; he will keep the goal of self-overcoming in mind and will never succumb to feeling sorry for himself or others.

C. Essay Questions

1. It is unlikely that you are an overman (or overwoman). But you now know a good bit about what such a person would be like. Imagine that you have arrived at that exalted status and are being interviewed on the following topics. What do you say to each?

- God
- values
- will to power
- eternal recurrence
- meaning in life
- equality
- selfishness

2. Nietzsche advises, become who you are, and Kierkegaard describes the human goal as being willing to be oneself. These sound remarkably alike, yet they must not be, for there are so many

differences between these two thinkers. Spell out the different ways in which they understand these phrases.

3. Suppose you are struggling with nihilism. Describe what that is like, and then review Nietzsche's prescription for dealing with it. Does it work?

CHAPTER 21

THE PRAGMATISTS
Thought and Action

ESSENTIAL POINTS

- Charles Sanders Peirce
  * Terminology: pragmatism, pragmaticism, practicalism, critical common-sensism, instrumentalism
  * Fixing Belief
    — Four methods: tenacity, authority, a priori, and scientific
    — Why none but the last will work; why that one works
  * Belief and Doubt
    — Belief as a habit; doubt as the lack of a habit
    — Critique of Cartesian doubt
  * Truth and Reality
    — Defining truth in terms of belief and doubt
    — All beliefs are entangled with others
    — It doesn't follow that we cannot know the truth of things
    — Truth as what a community of scientific inquirers will ultimately arrive at
    — Reality as what that truth says it is
    — Giving up the quest for certainty: fallibilism
  * Meaning
    — Restricted to intellectual concepts
    — Grades of clearness
    — Operational definitions
    — Contrast with Hume on meaning
  * Signs
    — Their triadic structure
    — Kinds of sign: indexes, icons, and symbols
    — Kinds of interpretants: emotional, energetic, and logical
    — The ultimate interpretant of a sign is a habit
    — How to attain more adequate habits

- John Dewey
  * The Impact of Darwin
    — Rescuing intelligence for practical ends
    — Getting over the old problems
  * Naturalized Epistemology
    — Intelligence as problem solving: the steps
    — Rejecting the representational theory: interactionism
  * Nature and Natural Science
    — Rejecting physics as the one unique representation of nature
    — Instrumentalism: concepts as tool; whatever works.
  * Value Naturalized
    — The modern problem: expelling values from nature
    — Value begins with likings
    — The difference between the satisfying and the satis-factory
    — The role of intelligence in valuation
    — Rejecting ends in themselves
    — Thought and action dependent on each other

TEACHING SUGGESTIONS

1. One of the key moves made by the pragmatists is their rejection of the representational theory of knowledge and perception. Though the chapter itself doesn't do this, a good way into it might be a review of that theory, together with its attractions, and a reminder of how dominant it has been in modern philosophy—accepted in large part by rationalists, empiricists, idealists, and skeptics alike. Replacing it with an interactive view of knowing is really quite revolutionary and has consequences for every part of philosophical thinking.

2. In a day when most students simply acquiesce in the common saying that we all have our own values, Dewey's thought that intelligence and scientific methods might be relevant comes as something of a shock. Make the most of it.

EXAM QUESTIONS
A. Multiple-Choice Questions

1. Peirce recommends the method of science for "fixing" belief because it
   - a. is more likely than other methods to get us true beliefs.
   - b. is the only way we can get certainty about the nature of reality.
   - c. is more precise than the others.
   - x d. attempts to improve our beliefs by testing them against something independent of ourselves.

2. What is it to believe something, according to Peirce?
   - a. To have a firm conviction about something.
   - x b. To possess a habit of acting in certain ways, given certain circumstances.
   - c. To have a habit that always makes you act in the same way.
   - d. To be disposed to say yes, if someone asks you if the world is round.

3. With respect to Descartes' procedure of methodical doubt, Peirce says,
   - x a. you can't really do that.
   - b. it's a good way to get the deck cleared for some serious intellectual work.
   - c. you don't need it to get to Constantinople and back.
   - d. it's a good mental exercise and prevents dogmatism and superstition.

4. As Peirce understands truth, it involves
   - a. noting the correspondence between what we say and what is real.
   - b. finding out what is real and then matching our beliefs to that.
   - x c. a community of inquirers.
   - d. the absolute certainty of knowledge.

5. In Peirce's theory of meaning,
   x a. signs always have a triadic structure.
   b. indexes are conventional signs.
   c. pragmatics deals with the word-world relationship.
   d. each sign must have a meaning independent of the meaning of every other sign, lest an infinite regress ensue.

6. Dewey offers us a naturalistic perspective in philosophy. By this he means:
   a. Human nature is unique in the world and we have to study it to understand ourselves.
   b. Physics, the basic science of nature, gives us the only true picture of things.
   x c. We are not spectators of the world, but involved participants in it.
   d. Values are naturally different from and opposed to facts.

7. Dewey's instrumentalism means that
   a. the instruments science uses are necessary to get the results it aims at.
   x b. ideas are tools in the service of practical ends.
   c. actions are means to ends.
   d. we may use other people as instruments to gain the satisfaction of our own desires only with their consent.

8. Dewey says that the life of the intellect is
   a. worth more than all the actions about which we usually busy ourselves.
   x b. basically one of problem solving.
   c. devoted to finding the eternal truths.
   d. an end unto itself.

9. According to Dewey, values are
   x a. subject to appraisal by scientific methods.
   b. not subject to appraisal by scientific methods.
   c. purely subjective and individual, so that we all have our own values.
   d. things we just like.

10. What is Dewey's account of the relation of ends and means?
    a. The ends justify the means.
    b. The means justify the ends.
  x c. There is a continuum of ends and means.
    d. Ends in themselves are the only things that can justify
       means to them.

B. Short-Answer Questions

1. What is belief for Peirce, and how does it differ from doubt?
    To have a belief is to have a disposition to behave in certain ways—
including saying certain things—given certain situations. To doubt is to lack such a
settled disposition, to be hesitant, unsure of what to do in those situations.

2. How does Peirce understand truth and reality?
    Truth is defined as the set of beliefs that persistent investigators, inquir-
ing according to the methods of science, would eventually come to agree upon.
Reality is what that set of beliefs says it is.

3. What method does Peirce recommend for settling opinion?
Why?
    Peirce recommends the method of science because it is the only one
that will work—that is, it will actually bring people to settled agreement about
things. It works because it is always trying to measure its beliefs against something that is independent of what people think it is.

4. How do Peirce's "clear ideas" differ from Descartes' "clear and
distinct ideas"?
    Descartes looks into himself and inspects the ideas in his mind. Are they
without obscurity, vagueness, ambiguity? Is each one distinguishable from all the
rest? Peirce, however, clarifies ideas by subjecting items to tests of various sorts
and noting the effects of these tests. An idea is clear when it can be defined in
terms of a set of definite hypotheticals expressing operations and results. So
Peirce's criterion for clarity is public and interactive, involving actions that set up a
habit, whereas Descartes' is introspective and private.

5. What does Peirce have to say about Descartes' quest for certainty in knowledge?
    Even if we were in possession of the truth, Peirce says, we could not
be certain that we were. For the truth is just what a community of inquirers would

145

ultimately come to agree upon, if they investigated sufficiently long according to scientific methods. It may well be that some of our beliefs will be in the set accepted in that ideal community, but that depends on how future inquiry—and science—goes. And we cannot predict that. The best we can do is work toward improving our beliefs by testing them in scientific ways, while relying on them so long as they don't disappoint us. We must be fallibilists.

6.   What is Peirce's critique of Descartes' project of methodical doubt?

Can't be done! It's no good just saying you doubt everything, while going on living—choosing and acting. Doubt is the absence of belief, and in the absence of belief you really would not know what to choose or to do. At all! So Descartes' doubt is a kind of fake. Anyway, there's no point to it, because as long as our beliefs work for us there is no motivation for doubting them.

7.   What does Dewey say is Darwin's impact on philosophy?

Darwin made it possible to think of life, including human life, as part of the natural world. And he replaced a fascination with eternal things by a concern for the way things change. So a philosophy informed by Darwinian science will not hanker after eternally unchanging first things but will concentrate on understanding and interpreting practical human concerns.

8.   Problem solving, Dewey says, is the heart of intelligence. How does he understand that process?

We are perplexed about something and try to get clear about the situation. Then we imagine a variety of possible solutions. In the light of those possibilities, we re-examine the facts; this may suggest other possibilities. We try out one and see whether it works to resolve the difficulty. If it does not, we try another and continue until we find one that is satisfactory.

9.   How does Dewey understand experience? Contrast it with an alternative?

Many philosophers have understood experience in terms of the internal life of the mind, thinking any relationship to external reality was inessential at best and perhaps totally irrelevant. Dewey, however, thinks of experience as a matter of interactions between an organism and its environment. It is active, ongoing, purposive, and anything but disinterested. From the start, experience is in touch with its objects.

10. Dewey says that value originates in likings, but that liking something doesn't mean it is valuable. Explain.

If we never liked anything, value (good, bad, right, wrong) would not even be on our horizon. In liking X we naturally think of it as good—desirable, valuable. But to think of it in this way involves a kind of prediction: that it *will* do. We need to examine X in the context of its conditions of acquisition and its consequences—that is, we should use intelligence (scientific methods) to find out more about it. If, knowing much more about it, we still like it, we can judge it is good (valuable). Of course, we still might be mistaken.

11. How does Dewey think means and ends should be related?

We should refrain from thinking there are ends-in-themselves that could justify any means to those ends. There are only ends-in-view—ends taken provisionally as ends. These are themselves means to still further ends; so there is a continuum of ends and means. This approach allows us to rationally criticize ends as well as means.

C. Essay Questions

1. Descartes sets himself to build up knowledge on a foundation of absolute certainty by doubting everything until he finds something he cannot doubt. Discuss this project from Peirce's point of view. Does knowledge have such a foundation? Does it need one?

2. Compare the representational theory of knowledge with a pramatic interactivist view.

3. Sketch Dewey's value theory, bringing in the notions of ends and means, truth, liking, and the uses of intelligence.

CHAPTER 22
ANALYSIS
Logical Atomism and the Logical Positivists

ESSENTIAL POINTS

- The linguistic turn in philosophy
- Language and Its Logic
  - * The idea of an ideal language
  - * Example: logic applied to definite descriptions
- Ludwig Wittgenstein: *Tractatus Logico-Philosophicus*
  - * A bit about his life
  - * The aim of the book: to set a limit to thought
  - * Picturing
    - — Possible states of affairs, facts, elements in a structure, pictorial form, logical form, logical space, and truth
    - — Why there are no pictures that are true a priori
  - * Thought and Language
    - — Thoughts as pictures
    - — Thoughts are expressible in language
    - — The essence of language is hidden, though present in every example of language
    - — Objects in relation are pictured by names in a structure
    - — The world is what is pictured in the totality of true sentences: all that is the case
    - — Simple sentences and complex: no logical relation between simple sentences; logical atomism
    - — The truth functionality of complex sentences
  - * Logical Truth
    - — Truth tables
    - — Tautologies and contradictions picture nothing
  - * Saying and Showing
    - — Propositions show their sense, say how things are
    - — The propositions of logic are all tautologies; they say nothing
    - — The propositions of logic are a priori knowable
  - * Setting the Limit to Thought

148

- There is a formula for generating every possible proposition from a set of atomic propositions
- What can be said is shown; what cannot be said is nonsense
* Value and the Self
  - The *Tractatus* has an ethical point, though such a point cannot be expressed in language
  - Ethics not a science; ethics is transcendental
  - The philosophical self
  - Why solipsism coincides with pure realism
* Good and Evil, Happiness and Unhappiness
  - Good willing is rewarded
  - The world of the happy man is a different world from the world of the unhappy man
  - Seeing life from the viewpoint of eternity
  - The problem of the meaning of life—the riddle—cannot be put into words; the problem vanishes
* The Unsayable
  - Philosophy as clarification
  - Climbing the ladder and throwing it away
  - Seeing the world aright; then—silence
• Logical Positivism
  * The verifiability principle of factual meaningfulness
  * The tautological character of logic and mathematics
  * The meaningless of metaphysics
  * The emotive meaning of ethical judgments
  * Problems with the verifiability criterion

TEACHING SUGGESTIONS

There was an abstract sculpture outside the room where I used to teach the *Tractatus*. I would draw a picture of it on the board, as exact as I could make it, but with one hole missing. The students never noticed the omission. I used it to explain the notion of picturing; all the details of Wittgenstein's account can find a home in such an explanation.

I presented it first as a picture of a fact. And then I said I had been lying to them, drew in the missing hole, and explained that it had been only a picture of a possible state of affairs. Something like this works well in making clear what otherwise would be pretty tough going for beginning students. With a good start like this, the rest is challenging but not impossible.

EXAM QUESTIONS
A. Multiple-Choice Questions

1. Russell's theory of definite descriptions
   a. explains the logic of phrases having the form, "The so and so."
   b. assimilates the logic of definite descriptions to the logic of names.
   x c. assumes that definite descriptions have meaning only in the context of a sentence.
   d. shows that definite descriptions are either true or false.

2. In Wittgenstein's Tractatus, every picture is taken to be
   x a. a fact.
   b. made up of elementary sentences "glued together" by logical words.
   c. a tautology.
   d. a picture of a fact.

3. The world, according to the Tractatus, is
   a. a very complex thing.
   b. all the possible states of affairs.
   x c. what would be pictured in the totality of true propositions.
   d. unknowable.

4. Language, in the Tractatus view,
   a. is composed partly of sense and partly of nonsense.
   b. says nothing, but shows itself.
   c. is obscure and needs to be reformed in the direction of an ideal language.
   x d. is, in the last analysis, composed of names in relation.

5. Tautologies, Wittgenstein tells us,
    x a. can be known to be true a priori.
      b. are pictures of very peculiar facts.
      c. show nothing.
      d. are sometimes true and sometimes false, and you need a truth table to tell you when one is the case and when the other.

6. Wittgenstein's main aim in the Tractatus is to
      a. explain the nature of language.
      b. give an account of how natural science is a priori knowable.
    x c. set a limit to thought.
      d. make accessible the results of the new logic.

7. About the part of the Tractatus that Wittgenstein did not write, he said that
      a. it is composed of nonsense.
    x b. it is the more important part.
      c. it deals with that part of natural science that remains to be discovered to this day.
      d. he would write that part in a subsequent volume.

8. Which of these sentences cannot be found in the Tractatus?
      a. "All propositions are of equal value."
    x b. "It is necessary for there to be propositions of ethics."
      c. "The world is independent of my will."
      d. "The world of the happy man is a different world from that of the unhappy man."

9. About the meaning of life, Wittgenstein holds that
      a. only science can help us here.
      b. language has so far been inadequate to the task of expressing it, but there is hope that it may be developed so as to succeed in solving the riddle.
      c. the riddle can be answered in the clear words of the *Tractatus.*
    x d. the solution lies in the vanishing of the problem.

10. About philosophy, Wittgenstein tells us:
    a. Its task is to tell us the truth about ourselves.
    b. It is not an activity but a body of doctrine.
x   c. It aims at clarity.
    d. When properly understood, it can be seen to be identical with science.

11. According to the verifiability criterion of factual meaning-fulness,
    a. propositions about God must be verifiable, because they deal with a factual question.
    b. the meaning of an ethical proposition consists in its conditions of verifiability.
    c. the criterion is itself verifiable.
x   d. nothing unverifiable can be meaningful.

12. Logical positivists
x   a. tend to take the "objects" of the *Tractatus* to be sense data.
    b. agree with Wittgenstein about the importance of the mystical.
    c. agree with Wittgenstein that ethical propositions express the feelings or sentiments of an individual.
    d. admit they are talking nonsense when they set out the conditions of meaningful language.

B. Short-Answer Questions

1. Sketch (in a general way, without all the details) how Russell's theory of definite descriptions can dispel confusion foisted upon us by misleading features of our language.

A definite description is a phrase of the form, "The so and so." Such phrases function rather like names and tempt us to suppose that if sentences containing them are meaningful, there must be some referent for the description. Russell showed that this assumption is misleading; he gave an analysis of sentences in which that linguistic form disappears, leaving behind existence assertions about things having certain familiar properties. This resolves logical puzzles and leaves us with clarity instead of confusion.

2. Why couldn't the "important" part of the Tractatus be written?

The important part had to do with ethics, value, and the good life. That part couldn't be written because it couldn't be formulated meaningfully in language. The reason is that the essence of language is picturing, and what is pictured in true sentences are the facts. Facts are valueless, and all alike. So matters of value and happiness simply cannot be expressed in language.

3. In the Tractatus, Wittgenstein held that a proposition is a picture. Explain this.

A proposition is composed of names in relation. Each name stands for a simple object. The relation of the names is structurally similar (has the same logical form) as the relation of the objects. Hence a proposition is a picture of a possible state of affairs; and if the objects are indeed related as the proposition says they are, the proposition is true and it pictures a fact.

4. In Wittgenstein's Tractatus, propositions are thought of as pictures. Very briefly,
    a. What do propositions picture?
    Possible states of affairs.
    b. What do tautologies picture?
    Nothing.
    c. What do true propositions picture?
    Facts.
    d. Can one elementary proposition entail another?
    No.

5. What is the world, according to the early views of Wittgenstein?

The world is all that is the case, the totality of facts (facts being objects in relation). It is what is pictured in the totality of true propositions.

6. Why do tautologies and contradictions "say nothing"? What do they do?

Tautologies say nothing because they shut out no logical possibilities; they don't exclude anything, so they don't picture one possible state of affairs rather than another. Contradictions say nothing because they shut out all logical possibilities; so they are not pictures either. What tautologies and contradictions do is to show, or display, the structure of logical space, within which facts and states of affairs reside. They also display the laws of logic.

7. How is the limit to thought set?

Thought is identified as what is expressible in language. Language is made up of propositions picturing possible states of affairs. Complex molecular propositions are truth-functions of elementary or atomic propositions. Wittgenstein found an operation on a set of propositions that would generate all the possible propositions (simple and logically complex) that could be formed from that set. Using that operation on the totality of elementary propositions yields everything that could be said—and so also everything that could be thought.

8. Is the philosophical self of the Tractatus more like Hume's fictional self or Kant's noumenal self? Explain.

It is not a fiction, though, like Hume, Wittgenstein cannot find it "in the world." It is more like Kant's noumenal self, with the exception that Kant believes it is possible to think it—have a concept of it—though we can't know it, and Wittgenstein holds that to try to express it in language at all is, strictly speaking, nonsense. "It" lies beyond the limits of the thinkable.

9. What is the task of philosophy, according to the early Wittgenstein? What is its correct method? Explain the ladder analogy.

The task of philosophy is the logical clarification of thought; it should not aim at producing theories or world-views, or true propositions. Its method should be to analyze what is said and show that if it is meaningful it belongs to natural science, and if it is not it is just plain nonsense. Wittgenstein's own work in philosophy should be treated as a ladder you climb up, until you see the world aright—and then you kick away the ladder. Strictly speaking, it, too, is nonsense.

10. Explain the verifiability criterion of meaningfulness and its consequences for ethics.

A proposition is factually meaningful, the logical positivists say, only if it can be verified—that is, only if some experience is relevant to determining whether the proposition is true or false. It looks like there is no experiential evidence that can be cited on either side for a moral judgment, so these are factually meaningless. There are no moral facts; however, such judgments may have another function, that of expressing how we feel about things.

11. What problems does the verifiability criterion run into?

The question obviously arises: Does it apply to itself? It doesn't seem to be verifiable by sense experience, so it can't be factually meaningful. Is it a definition? Well, it surely doesn't seem to capture the ordinary sense of meaningfulness.

So maybe it is a proposal as to what we would be well-advised to regard as meaningful. But then it is hard to see why we should accept it.

C. Essay Questions

1.   Contrast the view of value found in the pragmatists—for instance, in John Dewey's thought—with that in Wittgenstein's Tractatus.

2.   Compare the solution given for the problem about the meaning of life in Wittgenstein's Tractatus with Nietzsche's solution in terms of the overman and eternal recurrence.

3.   Compare Wittgenstein on the nature of value with the positivist's account of value judgments. Are there similarities? What are the differences?

CHAPTER 23
ORDINARY LANGUAGE
"This Is Simply What I Do"

ESSENTIAL POINTS

- We misunderstand our own language when it goes on holiday
  - Ryle and the myth of the "Ghost in the Machine"
  - Austin and excuses
- The Later Wittgenstein: *Philosophical Investigations*
  - Philosophical Illusion
    - The *Tractatus* ideal of a complete, exact analysis—of there being one single essence of language—rejected
    - The *Tractatus* prescribes to language; what we need is description
    - The baffling nature of philosophical problems
    - Philosophy leaves everything as it is; philosophy as treatment of an illness
  - Language-Games
    - Don't think, but look!
    - Primitive language-games illuminate features of language
    - The comparison of words with tools
    - Countless kinds of sentence—and the number is growing
  - Ostensive Definitions
    - We cannot enter the game of language via ostensive definitions; they are not the foundation on which language is built
    - Training
  - Objects
    - The meaning is the use (for a large class of cases)
    - Simple and composite are contextually determined
  - Family Resemblances
    - Many words do not have necessary and sufficient conditions for their use
    - There being no sharp boundaries is no hindrance to usefulness

- The Continuity of Wittgenstein's Thought
  * The opposition to "just *gassing*"
  * Setting the limit to thought
  * Showing what cannot be said: seeing the world aright
  * Giving philosophy peace
- Our Groundless Certainty
  * Obeying a rule
    — Grounded in a practice, a custom
    — The spade is turned; I follow the rule blindly
    — Agreement in language is rock bottom
  * Moore and common-sense truisms
    — We are certain of these, but we don't know them
    — Different language-games are possible
    — Justification comes to an end
  * The end of philosophy?

TEACHING SUGGESTIONS

1. To appreciate what Wittgenstein does in the *Investigations* it is important to have felt the temptation to *Tractatus*-like views. It is probably best, in light of this, to teach Chapters 22 and 23 as a package. In various guises, of course, a *Tractatus*-like package—a final solution, precision, well-founded belief, certain truth, a system encompassing everything, the viewpoint of eternity, the promise of happiness and absolute safety—has been found attractive by many in the long history of philosophy. So grasping the *Tractatus* is probably not absolutely necessary; but still—Wittgenstein's youthful classic puts all this very succinctly, making use of the best modern intellectual tools, and the first parts of the *Investigations* have it squarely in its sights.

2. Whether philosophy in many of its traditional concerns is no longer viable is a serious question that students should face. This chapter can help them face it.

EXAM QUESTIONS
A. Multiple-Choice Questions

1. Philosophers like Ryle and Austin advocate close attention to what we ordinarily say and when because
    a. people ordinarily tell the truth.
   x b. ordinary language has stood up to the long test of the survival of the fittest.
    c. Plato and Aristotle and Kant are too difficult for most people.
    d. ordinary language is perfectly precise, unlike the confusing language of the philosophers.

2. Wittgenstein now says that philosophical problems
    a. are deep, important, and real.
    b. can be solved if we bring to bear all we have learned from the previous history of philosophy.
    c. can be solved if we make use of the resources of modern science.
   x d. are like a disease.

3. What does the philosopher do, according to the later Wittgenstein?
    a. Entices the fly into the fly bottle.
   x b. Assembles reminders.
    c. Explains and deduces the answers to deep and serious questions.
    d. Changes everything.

4. Language-games show us
    a. that all words signify something.
    b. the essence of language.
   x c. how language is used in those practices where it has a home.
    d. that there are three basic kinds of sentence: assertion, question, and command.

5. Ostensive definitions, such as saying "spoon" while pointing to a spoon,
   a. are what allow children to enter the language-game of adults.
   b. give the word-world connections that supply basic terms with their meaning.
   c. are shown to be fundamental in language, contrary to the doctrine of the *Tractatus*.
   x d. can be variously interpreted in every case.

6. With the notion of family resemblances, Wittgenstein
   x a. shows us that many of our concepts are not bounded by strict rules.
   b. explains what causes parents and children to look alike.
   c. indicates that every word expresses the essence of what it is about.
   d. means to say that his book is like a photo album.

7. Early and late, Wittgenstein aims to
   a. do metaphysics with more precision than anyone has ever done before.
   b. improve on the way we normally speak.
   x c. give philosophy peace.
   d. construct a philosophical theory of language.

8. When we obey a rule,
   a. we should always consider the reasons for obeying it.
   b. that is something we could do once, and all alone, without anyone else even being capable of understanding what it is we are doing.
   c. we always have to decide what the rule means.
   x d. we obey it blindly.

9. When Wittgenstein says, "my spade is turned," he means that
   x a. justifications have an end.
   b. a conviction of his has been refuted.
   c. he was thinking in one way, and he now sees that he must think in another way.
   d. nothing is ever certain for us.

10. With respect to the claim, "There exists a living human body which is my body," Wittgenstein says that
    a. if I don't know that, I don't know anything.
    b. I know that with certainty.
x c. it is part of the inherited background against which he distinguishes between true and false.
    d. we should doubt even that.

11. When different language-games are being played, manifesting different world-pictures,
    a. a person in one game can give good reasons for the other to change her picture.
    b. each should check out his or her world-picture, to be assured of its accuracy.
    c. at least one of them must be mistaken.
x d. the participants can engage in persuasion, but not reason-giving.

B. Short-Answer Questions

1. In the Tractatus, Wittgenstein thought he had identified the essence of language: picturing. What does he now say about this?
    There is no essence of language. "Language," like "game" is a family resemblance word. There are "countless" kinds of language use, resembling and differing in endless ways, and new ones can always be added. We should not assume that because it is all called language, there is some one thing common to all these uses. Rather, we should look and see.

2. In the Tractatus, Wittgenstein identified the basic unit of language as a name and said that a name stood for a simple object. What does he say now about this?
    Not all words function as names—look and see! Moreover, when you do have a name, the object is not its meaning, or one couldn't meaningfully say that N.N. has died. Furthermore, ostensive definitions work only when a background of language use is already in place, so they cannot be the beginning of language. And language cannot be atomistic; the understanding and use of one concept necessarily involves many others. Finally, what is simple is relative to context and not itself something "simple."

3. In the Tractatus, Wittgenstein claimed that language was susceptible to a complete, exact analysis, using logic as the tool. What does he say now about this?

There is no one standard of exactness. Different levels are suitable for different purposes. Language does not everywhere have the crystalline structure of logic, nor need it have that, to do its varied jobs perfectly well. Look and see.

4. What is a language-game? And why is the study of language-games useful?

A language-game is an activity, a practice, a form of life involving language. It is useful to study language-games, including some simple cases, because it helps to illuminate the uses of words in those practices where they have their home. It is part of Wittgenstein's slogans: "Don't ask for the meaning, ask for the use," and "Don't think! Look!"

5. What does Wittgenstein understand by the term "family resemblances."

When there is no set of necessary and sufficient conditions for the use of a word, but overlapping and criss-crossing similarities exist among a number of features—some vaguely specified number of which constitute a word's meaning—he says its meaning is specified by giving these family resemblances.

6. What does the phrase, "This is simply what I do," mean for Wittgenstein?

This is what I say when explanations, justifications, and reasons run out—as they will. Here I have hit bedrock and can dig no deeper; my spade is turned. When I say this I am pointing to the form of life I live, to the practices in which I participate, to the world-picture that sets everything else in its place for me and cannot itself be sensibly doubted, justified, or known to be true.

7. In what sense do we obey rules blindly?

It is possible to give a reason for obeying a rule a certain way. And perhaps a reason, or justification for that. But reasons soon run out. And then we reach bedrock. We cannot get more firm foundations than are supplied in "what we do." That is, at the bedrock level we cannot see any farther. Justifications come to an end with our form of life. At that point, we obey "blindly."

8. What does it mean to say that our believing is groundless?

It means that our basic beliefs have a home in a world-picture or a form of life that cannot itself be justified. There is, contrary to the hopes of Descartes and many other philosophers, no foundation for knowledge and belief that is clear and distinct and certainly true. Justifications come to an end, and they come to an end earlier than most philosophers have wanted them to—in our practices, our customs, our language-games, our forms of life.

9. What are philosophical problems like, according to the later Wittgenstein?

They have the form: I don't know my way about. Things must be this way, we say. But then we say—they can't be that way! We are confused, baffled, unable to see clearly the lay of the land. A picture of how things must be may hold us captive, and we can't get out of it—everything we see seems to confirm its correctness but only because we see everything through it. We are under an illusion, often an illusion created by language—bewitched by misunderstanding our language.

10. What is the nature of philosophy, according to the later Wittgenstein?

Philosophy cannot give any explanations; it cannot prove anything; it cannot dig down to absolutely certain foundations and build on them. The most philosophers can do is assemble reminders of things we are already familiar with —but are distressingly apt to misunderstand. So the philosopher can be like a physician, curing the mental cramps we ourselves produce. He or she can help us find the way out of the fly-bottle.

C. Essay Questions

1. Compare the similarities and differences in Wittgenstein's treatment of language in the Tractatus and in the Investigations.

2. Suppose that Wittgenstein is right about what philosophy can and cannot do. What does that mean for philosophy as it has been practiced by rationalists, empiricists, and idealists for centuries?

3. When he ends by saying, "This is simply what I do," is Wittgenstein giving up on the quest for wisdom, or is he trying to reconceive what wisdom consists in? Explain.

CHAPTER 24
MARTIN HEIDEGGER
The Meaning of Being

ESSENTIAL POINTS

- What is the Question?
  - * What is the meaning of Being?
  - * The obscurity of the question due to the hiding of Being
  - * Being is not *a* being
- The Clue
  - * Being is always the being of an entity
  - * Dasein as the focus of the inquiry
  - * Ontic and ontological distinguished
  - * Being as an issue for Dasein
  - * An existential analysis, looking for the categories of existence: the existentials; fundamental ontology
- Phenomenology
  - * Disclosing Dasein's existence in its everydayness
  - * The hermeneutics of existing
- Being-in-the-World
  - * Dwelling
  - * The ready-to-hand and the present-at-hand
  - * Revealed in the ready-to-hand: nature, others, and the for-the-sake-of-which
  - * The genesis of objectification and the possibility of science
  - * The worldhood of the world
- The "Who" of Dasein
  - * Being-with as an existential
  - * Dasein as not differentiated from "the They"
    - — Distantiality and averageness
    - — The disburdening of Dasein
    - — The possibility of inauthenticity
- Modes of Disclosure
  - * Attunement revealed in moods
    - — Thrownness and facticity
    - — Anxiety as a disclosure of Dasein's having to be
    - — Falling away from oneself and into the They

* Understanding
  — Grasping possibilities; projection into the future
  — Interpretation and the hermeneutic circle
* Discourse
• Falling-Away
  * Idle talk: listening to and taking part in what-is-said
  * Curiosity: distraction
  * Ambiguity: understanding as "they" understand
• Care: the Being of Dasein
• Truth
  * Not a correspondence between two present-at-hand entities
  * Uncovering
  * Dasein as *in* the truth—and in untruth
• Death
  * Grasping Dasein as a totality
  * Dasein as Being-toward-death
  * Anticipation and authenticity
• Conscience, Guilt, and Resoluteness
  * Conscience is the call of authentic Dasein to Dasein lost in inauthenticity
  * A summons to Being-guilty
  * Anticipatory resoluteness as authentic existence
• Temporality and the Meaning of Care
  * Meaning as that wherein understandability maintains itself
  * Time as the meaning of Dasein's Being
• The Priority of Being
  * Why Heidegger's projected work was never finished
    — Too subjective
    — Too metaphysical
  * Understanding our age: technology
    — The way Being is given to us: as standing-reserve
    — Enframing as a mode of disclosure.
    — We did not choose this mode, and we cannot by taking thought change it
  * The extreme danger and the saving power
  * Art lets the truth happen
  * Being, time, and man: the event of appropriation
  * Letting Being be

TEACHING SUGGESTIONS

1. The forbidding terminology is not such a problem as it may at first seem. Once students get the hang of how that goes and see that Heidegger means to be describing them, they are eager to master it. It is all done rather abstractly, of course, so lots of examples help. If you mean to deal with Heidegger, though, you should leave plenty of time—a problem, sometimes, as it tends to come at the end of the term.

2. Heidegger is constantly in touch with the tradition as he thinks and writes. For this reason, he makes a good conclusion to this introduction. His "conversation" with Aristotle, Aquinas, Descartes, Kant, Hegel, Kierkegaard, and Nietzsche are especially salient. The similarity to the pragmatists on numerous points can be noted.

EXAM QUESTIONS
A. Multiple-Choice Questions

1. Heidegger chooses Dasein as the entity to interrogate as a first step toward uncovering the meaning of Being because
    a. he is not yet sure that anything else exists.
  x b. an understanding of Being is a definite characteristic of Dasein's Being.
    c. Dasein is a subject, and whatever has Being has it relative to some subject.
    d. he's got to start somewhere.

2. As Being-in-the-world, Dasein
    a. includes the world as a proper part of its own Being.
    b. exists primordially as present-at-hand.
  x c. is immersed in a world of gear or equipment.
    d. exists independently of others, with whom it must make connection if there is to be a common world.

165

3. In average everydayness, Dasein
   a. is the "I myself."
   b. is unconcerned with the "distance" between itself and the Others.
   x c. falls-in-with-the-One.
   d. is saddled with answerability for the way things go.

4. Anxiety
   a. needs to be overcome if we are to be authentic.
   b. reveals how far from the truth we have strayed.
   c. has as its object something determinately impending as a threat to Dasein's Being.
   x d. motivates falling-away-from-ourselves into the tranquilizing world of what "they" say.

5. "Falling-away-from" is characterized by
   a. an acute understanding of our inauthenticity.
   x b. fleeing in the face of anxiety.
   c. fleeing the world of the They.
   d. fleeing toward death.

6. In authentic existence, Dasein
   x a. anticipates its own death.
   b. finds its own pure essence, distinct from the they-self, and remains true to it.
   c. is true to its own understanding of itself as other-than-the-they.
   d. is motivated by curiosity to find the truth.

7. As Being-toward-death, Dasein
   a. necessarily flees-in-the-face-of-this-possibility.
   x b. can be understood as a totality.
   c. recognizes its guilt for not having done what it ought.
   d. identifies itself as something immortal, despite appearances.

8. The meaning of Dasein's Being, Care,
    a. is Being-itself.
    b. manifests itself in Dasein as worry-as-such.
    c. shows that the best thing for man is never to have been born.
x d. shows itself in having-been, making present, and being always ahead of itself.

9. Technology, Heidegger says,
    a is destined to destroy us.
    b. is the supreme danger but also the saving power.
x c. enframes things as being there for our use.
    d. positions man as the shepherd of Being.

10. In the event of appropriation,
x a. there will be a new sending of Being, a revealing in which the meaning of Being is not forgotten or hidden.
    b. man will appropriate the earth as sent for his use.
    c. Dasein will wrest the truth from its hiddenness by the power of its will and make it serve the potentialities of its future.
    d. God, too, will become standing-reserve and will satisfy all who authentically ask.

B. Short-Answer Questions

1. What is the problem Heidegger is concerned with, why is it a problem, and how does he propose to address it?
        The problem is the meaning of Being. It is a problem, he says, because we have disguised and hidden Being—our own included—and the philosophers have been busy helping. He addresses the problem by examining the Being of that entity for whom its own Being is an issue, Dasein. The method is phenomenological and hermeneutic.

2. Dasein is "ontically distinguished by the fact that, in its very Being, that Being is an issue for it." Explain.
        Among the beings that are, one is unique in having an understanding of its own Being; it matters to Dasein how it goes in its existence, and this is a matter of choice for Dasein. Since its own Being is open (or disclosed) to itself, it has

already a certain understanding of Being in general. We can interrogate Dasein as to how it understands its Being. The result will be a "fundamental ontology."

3. How does Heidegger understand Dasein's Being-in-the-world?

Dasein doesn't have the sort of Being that would allow it to doubt whether there is a world at all, as some philosophers have supposed. From the very first it is in-the-world, concerned with tools, gear, and equipment—the ready-to-hand. Dasein's involvement in this world reveals not only equipment, but also a world of nature and others like itself. The world is characterized by a series of in-order-to's that ultimately make reference to Dasein's concern for its own Being.

4. What does Heidegger mean by the "present-at-hand," and what is its relationship to scientific inquiry?

The present-at-hand is a mode of Being derivative from the more primordial ready-to-hand. It appears when the usual concernful use of gear is disrupted; it is characterized by disinterested or objective observation. Scientific attitudes regard objects as present-at-hand.

5. "Everyone is the other and no one is himself." Explain.

As thrown, Dasein is dominated by the One, the They. It falls-in-with the Others, understanding itself and how things go in the world the way "they" understand these things. This falling-in-with is tranquilizing and disburdening, relieving Dasein of the burden of responsibility for its own way of Being. Dasein also flees the anxiety of having to take up this burden, flees itself, and falls-away-from itself into the world of the One. This is inauthentic existence.

6. What are the main modes of disclosure for Dasein, and how do they turn inauthentic?

Attunement is Dasein's relationship to its own having-to-Be, and it shows up in moods. Moods show how Dasein is bearing the burden of having-to-Be-there. Understanding is a matter of grasping potentialities and interpreting them. Discourse puts things into words, expressing the articulation of Being.

Inauthentically Dasein expresses itself in idle chatter, gossip, and listening-to-what-is-said-in-the-talk rather than penetrating to the reality being talked about. Dasein degenerates into mere curiosity, a never-satisfied roaming about on the surface of things, and it tails off into ambiguity, where it is unclear whether anything is understood.

7. Can Dasein be understood as a totality?

Yes. The key is to see that Dasein is always unfinished, that there is always something of its Being that is still a potentiality, and then to see that there is one possibility that it cannot outstrip—death. So Dasein's Being is a Being-toward-death. In authentic existence, Dasein grasps this firmly in anticipation, not evading or denying it, or covering it up as "they" do. So Dasein stretches itself along between birth and death.

8. How does Heidegger understand conscience?

Conscience is a wordless call to Dasein to stop fleeing from itself into the world of the One and seize upon itself authentically. The call comes from Dasein itself and reveals Dasein as guilty—as not having been itself. It calls to responsibility, to resolutely taking up the burden of Dasein's thrownness and facing the potentialities that the past has made possible.

9. What is authentic existence?

Authentic existence is accepting one's thrownness and looking forward without blinking at one's potentialities—including one's death. In anticipation one grasps one's Being-toward-death, and with resolution one takes up responsibility for the self that one has become—guilty though that is revealed to be by the voice of conscience. So authenticity is not a mode of existence totally distinct from inauthenticity. It is rather a grasping of oneself as having-been, as projecting into a very specific future because of what one has been, and of living realistically in the present in the light of what one truly is.

10. What, according to the later Heidegger, is the essence of technology? Why is there something "monstrous" about that?

Technology is essentially a mode of revealing Being. In this mode, Being is revealed as "standing reserve," as ready for rational ordering, stockpiling, and use. There is something "monstrous" about experiencing everything in this way, because it assumes that everything exists for us—that we are the "lords of Being," rather than its guardians or shepherds.

C. Essay Questions

1. Descartes thinks that solipsism is a real possibility—one that needs to be ruled out by rational argument. Explain why he thinks this. Then discuss that claim from Heidegger's point of view.

2. Compare Heidegger's concept of thrownness-into-the-world-of-the-One to Wittgenstein's notion of the "picture of the world" that

forms the "inherited back-ground" against which we distinguish between true and false.

3. Is it correct to call Heidegger an "existentialist"? Give some reasons for thinking it appropriate and some for thinking it a mistake.

STUDENT PAPER TOPICS

THE PAPER

The quizzes and exams in this course concern how well you are understanding the thought of folks like Socrates and Aristotle. A paper will allow you to say where you now stand, after considering what they have had to say.

Such a paper will not require further reading or library research—though that is not ruled out. What it does demand is some serious thinking—thinking that demonstrates you have grappled with an issue of importance in the light of the best that has been written about it in the history of the West.

There are two broad topics on which you can write:

- the *best life* for a human being to live
- the best overall picture of *reality*

With respect to *one* of these topics,

1. choose a view expressed by one of our philosophers with which you *disagree*
2. *describe* that view accurately
3. construct an *alternative* that you think is better
4. present *reasons* (an argument, a *logos*) that you believe show that the alternative is better

In constructing your alternative and arguing for it, you may make use of any thoughts and arguments we have canvassed this term—provided you acknowledge their source. But this is not to be a *report* of "What Aristotle thinks of Plato's Forms" or "Why Augustine thought the Stoics were presumptuous." The aim of the paper is for you to *speak for yourself.*

Such a paper, then, will express your views, as they have come to be formulated under the pressure of "conversations" with the Sophists, with Socrates, the Skeptics, and so on. But a good paper will also display (1) an accurate and subtle understanding of philosophical issues and (2) skill in argumentation. So this will not be merely a "subjective opinion paper." Papers will be graded not on conclusions drawn, but on the adequacy of the understanding displayed and the quality of the arguments put forward.

This is not an easy assignment. A good paper will require much thought. Don't leave it until the last minute.

PAPER SPECIFICATIONS

On the last day of class, you will turn in a paper of seven to ten pages (typed, double-spaced, normal margins). Papers should be

- clear in intent
- well-organized
- persuasively reasoned
- impeccably written

With regard to the last point: proofread the paper, ask a friend to check for errors, use the spell-checker, and read it aloud to make sure each sentence makes sense. The paper will be graded *on these criteria*, not on whether the professor agrees with the arguments you put forward.

Unlike the quizzes and exams, this paper gives you a chance to express your own ideas and arguments, engaging the philosophers we have been studying by setting down some appreciations and some disagreements. The paper must show *understanding* of several philosophical positions and arguments; that is, it must not be the sort of thing you could have dashed off in an evening before you even took this course. However, it is not to be merely a *report* of someone else's ideas. It is to represent what you—at this time, after having studied Heraclitus, Socrates, Aristotle, and the rest—truly think on the topic assigned. This is your chance to play the philosopher!

Here is the topic. Many of you are looking forward to being parents some day; some of you may already be parents. Those of you who are not sure you want to be parents have a stake in the way your neighbors' children are raised. So, in five to seven pages, making use of what you have learned, address the topic:

> *Why I want my children (or my neighbors' children) to grow up to be, for instance, Stoics, Epicureans, Christian Aristotelians, a combination of Plato and Augustine, Cartesians, and so on— together with some philosophical errors I hope they will learn to avoid.*

Note that there are two aspects to this paper, a positive and a negative aspect.

"Victoria Boston has done it again! *3 Slow Nickels* is a story that you have to read when you want to be inspired and know exactly how to live your best life."

—Jonathan Sprinkles
Voted one of America's Top Speakers,
Author of multiple #1 Amazon Best sellers, Television Personality,
Founder of Presentation Power

"*3 Slow Nickels* will take you on a journey of success, filled with real-life disappointments, challenges, and adversity, yet provide practical advice and simple truth on how to overcome. After reading this book, you will walk away truly inspired and filled with hope so that you also, will become your best self and an inspiration to others."

—Coach Clint Crouch
Founder of Skills Society; former Assistant Coach for WNBA's Washington
Mystics and Director of Camps & Clinics Division of the
NBA's Washington Wizards

"Victoria Boston has wonderful advice for anyone looking for success in family, career, and life overall! Never handed a silver spoon, she built an amazing life and one that you too can have. *3 Slow Nickels* will inspire you and provide golden nuggets on how to do just that. Take the journey with her!"

—Kim Gandy
President of National Network to End Domestic Violence (NNEDV)

"Vicky Boston has real stories to tell and keeps it real in the process. Having overcome and beat the odds, she gives it to you straight and provokes self-determination. She inspires greatness in those around her and remains grateful and humble along the way. *3 Slow Nickels* is a must read! "

—Andrea Custis
Former Group President, Verizon Advanced Services

"Vicky Boston is that rare leader that brings the true potential out of her team through her unwavering personal courage, relentless pursuit of excellence, and unmatched ability to inspire employees at every level. While many leaders are busy "talking the talk", Vicky leads her team from the trenches, coaching her team through tough times, and celebrating success each step of the way. Vicky Boston is an inspiration and I am a better leader, husband, and father because of her influence on my life. You want to read *3 Slow Nickels*."

—Chris Arnold
Director of Operations, Verizon Wireless
Former Vice President of Alltel Communications

2/9/17

3 SLOW
NICKELS

Dear
Fredericia!
Thanks for all of
your support.
We ♡ you!
T + V

Author photos by Phelan Marc - www.phelanmarc.com
Stock images: Veer.com

ISBN-10: 0974154067
ISBN-13: 978-0-9741540-6-0
Also available as an ebook on Amazon.com.

Printed in the United States of America

Dedication

To my mom,
Louise Daniel Hutchinson

You were my incredible example when you were
here on earth and now that you're in heaven,
you're my guardian angel!

Table of Contents

Introduction

Photo: My parents and I at my brother's funeral. Hutchinson's were built for tough times...

How do you navigate a successful, rising career while maintaining a happy and stable personal life?

Every success story is filled with failures, disappointments, challenges, tears, sweat, and possibly even blood along the way. I intend to take you on a journey and share the lessons learned, pitfalls I avoided and crises overcome. Based on my humble beginnings, I never dreamed I could be a successful corporate professional, involved mom and wife, community volunteer and at times, even a committed full-time college student.

I started out in an entry-level position and ascended to a senior leader in a major corporation and learned along the way, sometimes by trial and error, how to balance my personal and professional life while staying true to my beliefs about what's important.

Think of this book as a series of personal mentoring sessions where you learn from my mistakes and successes and you leave with valuable nuggets of wisdom that you can take and apply to your own situation.

I grew up being mentored by my parents. I didn't realize it at the time, of course, but in retrospect, I see that my home environment was nothing short of an incubator for success — a breeding ground for excellence. To be perfectly honest, not only

did I not realize it at the time, I didn't always value it, appreciate it or embrace it. In this book, I pass on the wisdom that shaped me and the experiences and the mindset that resulted in my success.

I am the youngest of seven children and I watched my parents raise us in a small three bedroom house with one bathroom in one of the toughest, poverty-stricken neighborhoods in southeast Washington, DC — Anacostia. My parents taught us resilience and perseverance through adversity. As I watched my parents do what I perceived as the impossible, I learned the mindset of a champion. In fact, I learned that success is always on the other side of adversity when you refuse to quit or give up!

My parents buried one of my sisters, who died not long after birth, and my precious eight-year-old brother, after he was hit by a car on his way home from the playground. Though I was just three years old, I remember the strength they exuded during this stressful time in our lives. It impacted our entire community. They made an intentional decision that, rather than climbing into the caskets and dying with their children, they would live for them instead.

My parents worked every day and showed us first-hand what a real work ethic looked like. Their philosophy was if they didn't work hard, we didn't eat. As you can imagine, there were several mouths to feed including our dog, Fred (who was incredibly greedy) and cat, Morris who really looked like and was named afterthe one in 9Lives brand cat food commercials back in the day! I can't ever remember my parents calling out

sick for work or finding a reason to side-step any obligation. If they did, it was a rare occasion. They taught us at an early age that credibility matters — say what you mean and do exactly what you committed to doing. No excuses. I seldom witnessed my parents allow their race or gender to discourage them from being their very best self, although I'm sure it did at times. They seemingly gave their all regardless of endeavor and encouraged us to do the same.

My dad was tops in sales, and the first African-American salesman, at a prestigious furniture store. My mom retired as director of research for the Smithsonian's Anacostia Neighborhood Museum in Washington, DC and authored several books during her career. My siblings and I were without excuse. Where we lacked in money, college funds, material possessions, name-brand clothes and fashion, or fancy homes and cars, we never lacked in love, integrity, and hard work. It was in our DNA!

I developed an "it's all good" mindset as a result of experiences growing up as a Hutchinson. Hutchinsons didn't quit, refused to give up, and made a conscious decision to overcome. Hutchinsons played like champions and behaved as winners — period. This mindset didn't mean we wouldn't make dumb mistakes, fall off track, disappoint our parents, siblings or ourselves — because we most certainly did, but what it did mean was that we got up off the canvas, learned the valuable lesson and realized that it's all good, no matter what. As you can imagine, it wasn't always easy to embody this. There were times in all of our lives where we felt like quitting, giving up and forgot that we were champions. We

were highly encouraged to push through at every turn.

One of my favorite Nike quotes is: "Greatness has no peak. Willpower knows no obstacles. Quit making excuses, putting it off, complaining about it, dreaming about it, whining about it, crying about it, believing you can't, worrying if you can, waiting until you're older, skinnier, richer, braver, or all around better. Suck it up, hold on tight, say a prayer, make a plan and just do it." Every time I see it, it reminds me that no matter what — it's all good. There will always be a reason to quit, make an excuse, or doubt yourself and those around you. Whenever my mind shifts in this direction, I try to quickly remember that in the end, all things work together for good. Because I truly believe it's all good, I can simply execute the plan and just do it!

Not too long after my mom died, I remember having conversations with my dad and sisters, specifically about the impact she not only had on our lives but on all with whom she came in contact. We talked about her legacy and how we had to continue to live for her and carry on her good work – standing for what's right, encouraging others, giving in to purpose, and making a real difference in the world. It was in one of these uplifting conversations that my dad turned to me and said, "you know Victoria, there is a book inside of you." While most people who know me, call me Vicky, my father has always called me Victoria. "If I wanted to call you Vicky, I would have named you Vicky," he is known to say. He reminded me that my mother authored several books for the Smithsonian – *The Anacostia Story: 1608 to 1930, Anna J. Cooper: A Voice from the South* and *Out of Africa: West African Kingdoms to Colonization*, just to name a few. He

said to me that if my mother could write such amazing books, full of history and facts untold in the average classroom, yet essential to us knowing who we really are and where we came from, that certainly, I could pause and tell my story.

Now that I have lived a little, experienced a few setbacks, comebacks and level of success that I never imagined possible, I have the opportunity to share with you, in hopes that you too will connect to what's possible and quickly walk in the vocation to which you were called.

When you finish this easy-to-read, power-packed book full of actionable nuggets, my desire is that you will be inspired and equipped to fully engage in your life. Above all else, I want to offer hope. I want you to walk away knowing that there is something good out there just for you.

You can juggle demanding responsibilities successfully. You can be successful in corporate America and stay true to who you are. It CAN be done!

Ready? Let's go…

"Your only limit is you."

— Nike

Take a moment and jot down your perceived obstacles faced and be prepared to tackle them as you take this journey with me.

....

....

....

....

....

....

....

....

....

....

....

....

....

....

....

....

....

Rules of Engagement

Photo: #TeamBoston. Troy & Vicky celebrating 25 years of marriage.

As the youngest of seven children growing up in southeast Washington, DC, a neighborhood full of poverty, crime, alarming high-school dropout rates and pockets of hopelessness, I was always clear about the expectations in my household. I like to refer to my childhood home by its street number, 2415. Mom and dad were crystal clear on what behaviors and habits were acceptable at 2415. They were even more explicit on what would not be tolerated as a Hutchinson. The rules of engagement at 2415 were clear then and evident even now in my own household.

One of my parents' non-negotiable rules was that the bed should be made the moment you step out of it. This used to drive me absolutely nutty because I used to think it was pointless to make up a bed that you were going to eventually climb back into. This habit is so embedded in me (no pun intended) that, 40 years later, I'm still doing it. It's such an automatic response when I wake up that I even do it in hotels when I know there is staff compensated to do it for me.

My dad, Ellsworth W. Hutchinson, Jr., was former military and he worked several jobs until he found his true love – sales! In fact, he was the first African-American salesman at the prestigious Curtis Bros. Furniture store in Anacostia where he was #1 in sales year after year. In 1959, the furniture store commissioned Bassett Furniture to build the largest chair imaginable to be displayed in the parking lot of Curtis Bros. on

Martin Luther King Jr. Avenue. in Southeast Washington, D.C. A national historical landmark, it is affectionately known as "The Big Chair" and stands 19.5 feet tall, weighs 4,600 pounds and resembles a dining room chair made of African mahogany wood. George Curtis, the owner of the store, presented my dad with a black onyx ring with four diamonds and a big chair etched in the stone a result of his exceptional sales performance. At the age of 88, my dad still wears that ring today, more than 40 years later. By the way, all of his grandchildren have claimed that ring. What they clearly don't know is that I've already had that conversation with Dad! I guess we will all share and enjoy the coveted ring one day.

Etiquette is golden

My dad went on to excel in furniture sales until retirement and continues to be everyone's resident expert on mattresses. Because of his love of sales and the pure enjoyment of instantly connecting with everyone he comes in contact with, it took three acts of retiring before he finally hung up the jersey at the precious age of 83. I believe this is exactly where I get my natural salesmanship and ability to connect with others! A few of my dad's most critical rules of engagement were and still are:

- Always be on time, in fact be early.
- Always keep your word; never break a promise.
- Be kind to everyone because relationships matter.

As I previously mentioned, my mom was an educator, historian,

researcher for the Smithsonian, author and community activist. She was the voice for those without one and always took a stand for what she believed was right for her family and for the community where she lived and served until her passing in the fall of 2014. As I reflect on my childhood, I recall that my mom worked a lot and probably could have done a better job paying attention to her own health. In today's health-conscious environment with fitness centers conveniently located near shopping centers and an overload of information on healthy eating and natural remedies, it seems easier to incorporate a fitness regimen into our modern lives. Unfortunately, that wasn't the case for my mom.

Still, she was very smart and witty with exceptionally high standards for herself and everyone she encountered. Her core belief was that failure was not an option and that regardless of color, class, gender, or economic status, we, her children, had everything we needed to be successful. Excuses of any kind were not accepted in our home as a child and even after we moved and started families of our own, she continued to remind us of this. Of course, we made mistakes, but the use of the word "can't" wasn't entertained or tolerated EVER! She even convinced us that the word "can't" wasn't in the dictionary.

When we did make mistakes, she was right there to encourage us to quickly learn from them. Oddly enough, learning the difference between making mistakes and not making excuses was difficult for me to wrap my head around as a young adult. Seemed like whenever I made a mistake, I had a ton of excuses for why it happened. I think what my mom was trying to

teach us was that, even though we are created in the image and likeness of a perfect God, we as humans are far from perfect. Hence mistakes would be made; however, we were expected to learn from them. I grew up being super-competitive, critical of and hard on myself. It wasn't until later in life that I stopped beating myself up when I failed. Like any child, I never wanted to disappoint my parents. I struggled to differentiate between giving my best and sometimes falling short and failing because I simply didn't give it my all. There's a big difference between the two.

A book for idle hands

My parents strongly believed that education was our currency. They wanted us always to keep a book in our hands. But not just any book. They encouraged us to read books that exposed us to ideas, thoughts and places that we may not have yet experienced. While we may not have been thrilled at the onset, the habit of constantly reading certainly added to our curiosity! If we ever grumbled that we were bored, we knew a book was coming directly our way. It's so hard to admit this knowing my mom was an author and had such a love for books, but I actually did not start enjoying books of any kind until I was well into my 20s. As a child and a young adult, reading always felt like a chore. Now, I always keep a book in my hand. What started as a dreaded duty, is now a joy.

In elementary and junior high school particularly, my school principals and teachers were often times my mom's best and closest friends. As a result, the teachers were tougher on us in

class. While it may sound great now that my parents, especially my mom, knew almost every educator in the city, it surely didn't seem great then. They all kept a close eye on us. It really didn't seem fair at the time; we had no idea how much of a blessing it was to have such involved parents in our education and school system overall.

The neighborhood where we grew up, and where my dad still resides, was very close knit. The neighbors were well aware of the standards that Louise Daniel Hutchinson set for her children – the Hutchinson Clan. Whether home, at school or playing in the neighborhood, we were consistently held to the highest standard. I can remember a time in the 6th grade when an oversized classmate who was the known bully attempted to take my lunch during recess. At the time, I had a red metal Wonder Woman lunch box with a black shiny handle. (I wish I held on to it because it's going for $250 on eBay today!) Bologna and cheese was my favorite sandwich with chips and a drink. On special occasions like birthdays or when I received exceptional report cards, I looked forward to a Chips Ahoy chocolate chip cookie as an extra treat! On this particular day, the bully approached me on the black top. The black top is where we practiced track after school, but it also doubled as the hang out area during lunch recess when the weather permitted. While I don't remember all the details of the exchange, what I do remember and likely never will forget is having to defend myself after being shoved and told to relinquish my lunch and favorite (and only) lunch box. Rather than cave to her demands, I hit her in the head with my metal lunch box and as a result she required stitches. The incident spread like wildfire at school, home and in the neighborhood.

I can remember receiving multiple lectures from my homeroom teacher, parents, the adults in my neighborhood, and the principal on how violence doesn't solve anything and that I should have alerted an adult at the onset of being picked on instead of taking matters into my own hands. I can especially remember my principal saying, "Hutchinsons don't behave this way." Of course, my oldest sister applauded my efforts and condoned my behavior. She was all about self-defense at all costs! Growing up in a neighborhood like ours, you were constantly playing out in your head how you would defend yourself to and from school as well as when we hung out at the Fort Stanton neighborhood recreation center – now refurbished with a community room named after my mom.

Moms know best

None of the advice on keeping the peace and telling an adult seemed to make sense to me at the time but years later, I found myself giving that same advice to my daughter when she was in the 2nd grade. My daughter's school went from kindergarten through 8th grade, which meant she rode the school bus with children up to 14-years-old. I can still hear myself saying, "Remember, Danielle, if anyone bothers you on the bus, let the bus driver know." But in the back of my mind, I was thinking how I stopped that bully in her tracks handling things my way.

In hindsight, my mom knew best. She knew the potentially devastating effects of allowing our environment to define us. Poor choices in friends could derail us. Allowing the streets to

be our teacher could literally kill our purpose and potential, if not our mortal bodies. Many of mom's words of wisdom reverberate even now, especially these nuggets:

- Reading is not optional; lifelong learning is a requirement.
- Never quit, never give up.
- Know who you are, know that you are loved, and live out your purpose.

The Hutchinson rules of engagement absolutely helped shaped me into the disciplined person that I am today. As you reflect on your life and upbringing, what are the things that shaped who you are? What are the values that you live by?

....

....

....

....

....

....

....

....

Good fences

It's vitally important to establish the rules for your home and family, even if your family only consists of one member — you! There will always be competing interests, and it is essential that you establish these principles before problems crop up.

Author, Teri Johnson, a licensed mental health counselor with a masters in psychology, has written extensively about relationships and suggests that success in marriage comes from identifying, clearly articulating and executing boundaries, or what I call rules of engagement. Boundaries are viewed as fences around our homes and those boundaries inform those governed by them, she says. The boundaries help others around us know what's expected if they choose to come inside the fences of our lives. Establishing the rules of engagement is a constant work in progress, says Johnson. As with anything, there are seasons in our lives — marriages, starting a family, buying a home, careers, and the aging process. Thus, the rules may be fluid and dynamic versus static.

As I transitioned from my childhood home at 2415 to my own home, 6010, I too wanted to ensure that there were clear rules of engagement, established for my own home and family. My husband always had high standards for himself and when I became Mrs. Troy P. Boston, we wanted the Boston family to live by a certain creed:

- Bostons are strong.
- Bostons don't quit.

- Bostons finish what they start.
- Bostons are credible.
- Above all else, Bostons put God and family first.

Regardless of my position, title or responsibility at work or in the community, nothing and no one came before the Boston clan at 6010. That was the goal, anyway, to put family before career, and sometimes I hit that goal and sometimes not so much.

Looking back, I can see that the rules of the house that my husband and I created — rules we created based on what was really important to us — kept us grounded and centered. We never really wrote the rules down or posted them around the house. We discussed them as a family in casual settings, lived them out, modeled the behavior and challenged one another when we veered off course. It seemingly became second nature, our unwritten standard operating procedures.

For example, one of my favorite rules was not going to bed angry (easier said than done). Even if we were angry with someone outside of our household, we encouraged each other to resolve whatever issue we had. As we liked to say, "squash the beef" before bedtime so as to not carry today's drama into tomorrow.

Family before career

Before making any decisions regarding a new position, career move, promotion, relocation opportunity, new responsibilities at work, or volunteering in my community, I would weigh the impact it would have on my home life.

I strived to make every decision with 6010 in mind. Yet, I remember a time when I made the decision to live apart from my family to accept a job hundreds of miles away, one that likely would have been catastrophic for my family relationships. I frequently discussed my career mobility with my husband, or at least I thought I was having what I considered frequent conversations. I worked for a national firm where employee relocations from state to state happened all the time.

However, this near-miss happened when I failed to consider everything that was going on, not only in our immediate home but with our parents and grandparents. It's funny how when you really want something, you can justify anything! This was the case when I was twice offered a promotion by a very senior leader who had a reputation as one you really wanted to work for if you aspired to attain career mobility and growth. The first time the promotion was offered, I declined it because of bad timing and now the question was back on the table. The only real dilemma for me was that the job was in Tampa, Florida, at the time. While mobility was a topic often discussed at home, there was something that I hadn't fully factored into the situation: my mom and my mother-in-law's health had both begun to decline. In a selfish moment, I was able to initially sell my husband on the idea that this was a great opportunity and one that I shouldn't pass up again. After all, I had worked hard and deserved it, or at least that is what I told myself. Being the salesperson that I am, I convinced everyone that this was a great idea!

Troy and I had decided that for this particular opportunity, if I

accepted the promotion, I would move down to Tampa alone and commute back to the DC area a few times a month. He and Danielle would stay back to avoid disrupting her schooling and his career. I really wanted this promotion and even more so the chance to work for a dynamic leader.

To complicate matters, I had some so-called mentors whispering in my ear, "Vicky, if you turn this down, they will NEVER offer you another promotion. You would be crazy NOT to take this." I was afraid that refusing the promotion a second time would mean lights out – career suicide.

As you can imagine, I had a huge decision to make. Although, I seemingly had the support of my husband (not so much from our daughter), something just wasn't sitting right with me. However, I accepted the promotion. Within 24 hours, it hit me that my decision was all wrong. How could I leave my husband, who is an only child, to care for his sick mother, care for our teenaged daughter and help my siblings with my ailing mother, while I was hundreds of miles away?

We all knew that every time I got a new position, I would dive in full bore the first 90 days to get my arms around it. The idea that I would bounce back and forth between DC and Tampa was neither reasonable nor realistic. But the wheels for my relocation were in motion. In my mind, it would most certainly mean career suicide to have a change of heart and turn it down at this point. It was only when I remembered one of the Boston family's core values, God and family first, that sanity and serenity returned. Looking back, I have no doubt that moving to Tampa

at that time would have been catastrophic for my family. It would have been undue stress on Troy, which would have no doubt put a heavy strain on our marriage. Not long after, my mother-in-law passed. I am eternally grateful that I was where I was supposed to be at the time my family needed me.

As it turned out, this critical decision wasn't career suicide after all. I received promotions thereafter. In fact, this wasn't the last time I turned down a great opportunity due to poor timing for my family. A few years later, I had the chance to take an assignment in Basking Ridge, New Jersey, near my company's headquarters. The position, while not a promotion, was a lateral move that would have positioned me for tremendous visibility by the chairman. The way the team was set up back then, this position reported to a vice president who answered to a senior vice president who reported directly to the chairman. Having gained some wisdom and strength from the previous experiences, I was able to really think it all through, discuss it with Troy, Danielle and other close family and friends. In the end, while everything looked great on paper, especially as it related to career upward mobility, it came down to what was the best decision for 6010 overall. Without any hesitation or ambiguity, I thanked the leaders for the consideration and job offer, explained my family situation which included my mom's further and rapid health decline, and respectfully turned down the position.

Consider the costs

Think it through, remembering your established rules of

engagement, and consider the cost of the decision as well as the long-lasting consequences!

Don't wait until a job offer or other life-altering opportunity presents itself to initiate or have "the conversation." Talk to your spouse, close family, and/or significant other regarding life-altering opportunities that can cause shock waves throughout your home and personal life.   Oftentimes, the shock waves come because you haven't discussed things that could happen before they happen. The benefit and advantage of having "the conversation" ahead of time is to avoid the surprises and not to catch anyone off guard. This can be very problematic on all fronts. When you're not sure about your mobility, ability to relocate the family and/or ability to travel, it can cause you to waffle in your decision-making at work and at home. It can also cause you to be viewed as indecisive by the person offering you the opportunity.   Knowing in advance if you're able to relocate your family, with or without restrictions, and if you are able to travel, whether with limited or advance notice, is super important. It was my goal to have "the conversation" quarterly or as often as needed to avoid surprises. I also kept my leadership team informed so they were just as clear on my status and limitations, if any existed. Once you are crystal clear about your "6010," the rules of engagement and boundaries for your home life, you can be clear with everyone else. Clearly set expectations.

Have the conversation

While we may not have always nailed all the rules at 6010, the

Bostons set some lofty goals:

- Put nothing before God and family — period.
- Ask and know what is important to each other and seek to support it; whatever "it" is.
- Make decisions as a family and consider the impact on 6010.
- Be on time and keep your word. Commitments matter.
- Communicate, communicate, and communicate some more – NO secrets!
- Be willing to sacrifice for the greater good.
- Embody the Team Boston mindset – we all have on the same jersey.

Dwight D. Eisenhower said, "We succeed only as we identify in life, or in war, or in anything else, a single overriding objective and make all other considerations bend to that one objective." One of my mentors, Jonathan Sprinkles, often says it this way – "know what bows to what and know what is absolutely first and then second." What is your one objective that you will ensure everything else bends or bows to support it?

Take a moment and consider the following questions to help you define and support your "6010."

What's most important to my family?

....

....

....

....
....
....

2. What are our family goals?

....
....
....
....
....
....

3. Am I making decisions today to help us achieve the family goal(s)?

....
....
....
....
....
....
....

4. Have I had "the conversation" with my family, loved ones and those in my support system about mobility and the ability to travel for work?   Yes/No

    a. Am I mobile?

....

....

    b. What are my limitations (i.e. Can I relocate the family domestically but not internationally, East Coast only, etc.)

....

....

....

....

....

    c. If I am not mobile now, when will I be?

....

....

....

....

....

....

d. Can I travel with limited to no advanced notice and ensure family support is in place?

....

....

e. If able to travel, is it limited to 25%, 50% or 75%? Do I have the infrastructure in place to support a job with 100% travel requirements?

....

....

....

....

5. As it relates to relocating and/or travel, what are the deal breakers for my "6010"?

....

....

....

....

....

....

....

....

If it's been a while since you've had "the conversation" or perhaps you've never had this talk with your family, significant other, loved ones and those in support, today is a great day to get "the conversation" started. It's up to you to ensure your "6010" is set up for success, provided for and protected at all costs.

Make a date to get "the conversation" started.

"Never apologize for having high standards. People who really want to be in your life will rise up to meet them."

— Unknown

Drop the Guilt

Photo: January 1, 2015 - A mother's kiss before her daughter's wedding. Being there when it matters most...

My daughter, Danielle, is a very successful and productive adult, now happily married. She graduated from Pepperdine University in three years with a bachelor's degree in communication, marketing and advertising. She and her husband, Dion, are professional dancers, choreographers and actors who run a nonprofit organization serving underprivileged youth in Compton, the hard-scrabble Los Angeles suburb known for gangsta rap where Dion was born and raised. At such young ages, Danielle and Dion have traveled the world and toured with some of the biggest names in the entertainment industry, including Beyonce, Mariah Carey, Will.i.am, Usher, and many more. Their passion to give back to their community is the motivation for the great work they are embarking on today. I beam with pride at the daughter my husband and I raised. To see the accomplished, compassionate woman she has become puts everything into perspective. If I had any doubt before about whether or not I was at home enough, those questions don't loom as large in my mind anymore. I gave her the very best pieces of me — Boston family values and ethics and an abundance of nurturing and love, and I think her life reflects that. So if you were to ask Danielle was I home when she lost her first tooth, chances are she wouldn't remember and as she nears age 27, she likely doesn't care.

But you couldn't convince me of that when I was working late one evening to prepare for a big meeting the following day, and I got "the call" from hubby that her first tooth had fallen out!

OMG, I was guilt-ridden and thought I was going straight to hell that moment for missing such a major milestone in my one-and-only child's life.

This wasn't the first time I was overwhelmed with guilt and wouldn't be the last. How about the time I missed her dance recital in the 7th grade when she had a solo and huge part in the production? Or the time when she wanted both mom and dad to accompany her class on the pumpkin patch field trip? Then, there was the basketball game when she was the starting point guard and, of course, with so much always going on, I had the location of the gym wrong and missed half if not almost the entire game!

I really thought life was over when my flight was delayed out of the dreaded Newark, New Jersey, airport and I missed my daughter's 12th birthday. Every birthday is a big, darn deal in our house, only because I always tried to make it so. But this was the BIG 12th birthday! Troy and I had made plans to take her to dinner to celebrate being on the verge of teendom, but due to circumstances beyond my control I would not be able to make her birthday. Seriously, was the world really coming to an end? Of course not, but I had worked myself up and had actually convinced myself that I was the worst mom in the whole wide world for missing such a special day, as if it couldn't be celebrated or acknowledged at some other point in time. It's so cool that I can actually laugh at this today, but at the time, there was so much unnecessary drama!

I was frantic when I realized that there was no way that I was

going to get home in time for her birthday dinner. Very calmly, my husband said, "No worries, I will just pick up Charnee' (her best friend at the time) and take them to Dannie's favorite restaurant. It will work out fine." Finally, it hit me to drop the self-imposed guilt and redirect the negative energy consuming me and focus only on what I could control. I contacted Troy and asked him to have the waiter bring dessert to the table after dinner and call me so I could sing happy birthday by cell phone. Of course, this was long before Skype and FaceTime. My husband wasn't actually thrilled about this idea because he knew I was making this way bigger than it needed to be. My daughter understood when he explained the flight delays and was happy her best friend was able to join her on a school night. Even though both Troy and Danielle understood and didn't express any disappointment, I couldn't help but feel like I let them down.

After several experiences like this, I decided to ask my daughter, who was very active in extra-curricular activities and sports, what events and activities were most important to her. I also asked my husband, who volunteered weekly at our local church and coached boys basketball, what events and activities were most important to him. He was extremely supportive of my career and I wanted to be sure I was making every effort to support what was also important to him. This one conversation changed everything! Activities that I had elevated to high-priority status, in some cases were lower on the totem pole, and other things they were involved in that seemed less significant in my mind ended up being a big deal to them. The process of talking this through, actually taking the time to flush it all out, alleviated so much stress. It felt like it added ten years back to

my life.

For the critical dates and events that they identified like the spring dance recital with a solo role or the basketball game that determined if the team advanced to the playoffs, I moved heaven and earth to be there. For those games, track meets, field trips, and dance recitals I could attend as well as those I could not, I ensured there was always an army of fans and full-blown cheering section made up of family, friends, and neighbors who loudly chanted "go Boston" and supported the cause!

Being strategic, asking what was important to them, and taking the necessary steps to make it happen, made all the difference. Here's the deal, even if I fell short from time to time (and believe me, I did) and was unable to make all the family events and activities deemed important, they appreciated the fact that I tried everything in my power to make it happen. Obviously, I still missed some critical dates but my network of supporters and extended family certainly helped to make up for my absence.

The everything calendar

One of the big lessons here was to put pride aside and ask for help. I found that too many times, I was trying to make it all happen and nearly killing myself in the process. At other times, I was simply moving too fast and forgetting to add critical dates to the calendar, which caused unnecessary confusion. This taught me to slow down a bit and take time out every Sunday to do a calendar review as a family to ensure that we were all on the same page. Sometimes, there were just too many moving

parts to memorize who's on first base and who's on second! To this day, I put everything on the calendar and couldn't manage life without it. Forget having a separate personal and business calendar; that quickly became way too complicated. One calendar with everything – doctor appointments, back-to-school meetings, dance rehearsals, birthdays, anniversaries, big meetings at work and more. You get the point. EVERYTHING goes on the calendar. If it wasn't in writing, it probably would not get done.

Another lesson learned was remembering to explain "why" I would miss an important event to help ease the disappointment. If I knew I was not going to be able to make a dance recital, school play, family dinner or anything important to our family, I would explain the scheduling conflict in advance, especially to my daughter, and would reassure her of the support that would be there. She quickly understood when I took the time to break it all down, although hardly ever pleased (understandably so). Every blue moon, she would ask why I had to be the one who had to fly here and there to meet with a customer or why I had to work late to fix a problem. Truthfully, I didn't expect her to always get it. Heck, sometimes, I asked myself those same questions! Why me?

There were some field trips that she really wanted me to chaperone, and others weren't such a big deal at all. With limited vacation days each year, and having a very demanding job that required tons of travel, negotiating became a regular occurrence at 6010! One of the strategies I quickly embraced was measuring out vacation according to school activities. My

annual leave was mostly eaten up by the school calendar, so we tried to schedule our family vacations around spring break each year as well as bank a few vacation days for the unexpected. With Troy and I both working for utility companies, they seldom closed for inclement weather. In fact, our companies really didn't close for anything. As a result, we required a long list of backup supporters that we could call on in a pinch for school and family emergencies in case one or both of us couldn't make it.

I am very grateful for the unconditional love and support Troy provided during my career journey. We didn't really sit down at any point during our careers and plot out who would go after the promotion or whose career would need to take a back seat. We were very fortunate that our career paths complimented each other and overall supported the needs of the family. For many years, Troy worked out in the field as a senior technician for Washington Gas, a local utility company. He loved his flexible schedule which allowed him to make schedule changes as needed when I was away on business travel. Thankfully, Danielle was never a latchkey child. It was important to us to have one or both parents at home in the evening after school to assist with homework and to prepare dinner. Later in our careers as we both progressed, we discussed the opportunities and the impact on our family. Fortunately, the promotions Troy accepted still allowed him to pick up much of the slack at home, such as preparing dinner, ensuring Danielle made it to evening dance rehearsals, keeping the house clean, laundry and so much more. Troy successfully led and continues to lead a great group of technicians and staff supervisors and is responsible for the gas pressure for his territory in Prince George's County, Maryland,

minutes outside of Washington, DC. We always approached our marriage and family responsibilities as a partnership and I can honestly say, it was nearly an automatic response when one of us needed to step up in a bigger way to support the other.

Vince Lombardi said, "Once you agree upon the price you and your family must pay for success, it enables you to ignore the minor hurts, the opponent's pressure and the temporary failures." I couldn't agree more, and it was most liberating the day I learned to drop the guilt!

Quality time matters

Go through the steps of asking your loved ones what's important to them and understand what's important to you as well. You just might find that what you suspected was a big deal to your family and friends, may not be after all. Because I traveled most weeks for work, I made a concerted effort to visit my parents on Sundays. I would get so frustrated with myself if I couldn't spend the entire afternoon with them because I assumed, without asking, that's what they wanted. One Sunday afternoon when I was visiting with my parents, an issue arose at work. I was on a call in an attempt to get the situation resolved and after hanging up the phone, my mom said in a very kind yet sarcastic voice, "When you're in my house visiting, stay off your cell." In other words, she wanted me in the moment with her even if the moments were short. I learned really quickly that it wasn't the duration of my visit that mattered at all but ensuring the time was well spent and meaningful. Who knew? Prior to that encounter, I had never asked either mom or dad what was truly

important to them when I visited.

The "so what" of all of this: Stop wasting energy on guilt. Take a moment and just find out what's important to those you care about and those who care about you. What are you feeling guilty about today? I challenge you to journal it below. After you get it on paper, whatever it is, I now challenge you to simply let it go!

....

....

....

....

....

....

....

....

....

....

....

....

....

....
....
....
....
....
....
....
....
....
....

"You were put on this earth to achieve your greatest self, to live out your purpose, and to do it courageously."

– Dr. Steve Maraboli

Finding Balance

Photo: My great-nephew, Caden, catching his balance! You really can have it all... perhaps, just not all at the same time.

While attending a women's leadership conference several years ago in San Francisco, one of the panelists really stood out to me. This speaker was of special interest to me because at that time she was CEO of the Oakland Raiders, the first and only female "C" level executive in the male-dominated NFL. Her name is Amy Trask. She retired from this position back in 2013, not too long after I had the pleasure of hearing her speak. Her golden nuggets and overall remarks at the conference have stayed with me and I refer back to them often. I can remember the question-answer part of the panel discussion so vividly, especially the infamous question about how to balance work and home life (which seems to come up at nearly every conference I attend). I remember someone asking Amy specifically, how someone in her position, with so much responsibility, visibility and history in the making, balance work, home, community, fun, personal development, and of course the "S" word - sleep. I recall her simple yet profound response that made such a big difference in my life and in the way I viewed my own work-home life balance (or should I say, my struggle with the perfect balance).

Amy responded that she clearly communicated to her family, friends and loved ones that during football season, all bets were off. My interpretation of her comments was that she was upfront about her demanding work schedule and what her family and others who depended on her could count on during the season. I also remembered her sharing how she intentionally made

herself super available during the off season and that, in fact, was her balance. I realized in that moment, that we all have to figure out our own balance equation. What works for one working mom, dad, or family, may not work for others. When my husband and I decided early on to define what "6010" meant to us, it was an attempt to strike a healthy balance in our home life.

Depending on the seasons in our life, some things that used to be deal breakers, like eating together as a family when my daughter was much younger, did not hold the same weight when she was in high school and had a crazy school and extracurricular schedule. As I reflect back to the early days of my marriage to 25 years later, one of our non-negotiables that remains in place today is worshiping together as a family at our local church. Now that my daughter is grown, married and living clear across the country, whenever she and our son-in-law come home to visit, they, too, look forward to attending Sunday morning service with us. This is one that has always been super-important to us and has sustained us as a family.

Tackling defeat

I had Danielle when I was 19, right out of high school. Needless to say, that made it a little challenging to attend college full time. I tried to take a few classes here and there and failed miserably. At the time, I wasn't organized enough nor mature enough to balance all of that simultaneously. I can remember one of the counselors at my community college saying to me that I was simply wasting money since I had only passed maybe two out of

eight classes. I felt defeated and quit on the spot. I had bouts of starting and stopping and always had a great excuse for quitting. Wow, the more I think about it, I had actually perfected the art of quitting. At least, I had convinced myself that the excuses were good reasoning. When my daughter was in the 6th grade, her teacher asked her to memorize a poem and share it with the classroom. Here's an excerpt from it:

> "Excuses are tools of the incompetent which create
> monuments of nothingness.
>
> Those who specialize in them
> are seldom good in anything..."
> —*Author Unknown*

There are many versions of this poem; however, these are the lines that I clearly remember Danielle repeating around the house over and over until memorization set in. I'm not sure what triggered the teacher to share this poem, but, I believe it wasn't by happenstance that my child was charged with learning it. To this day, I believe that poem was for me. It was in those moments that I was very comfortable with my ongoing excuses to quit school and had no regret. The words in this poem challenged my complacency.

Even though the poem had a profound impact on my life, I didn't make changes in my life instantly. As you can imagine, I started and stopped a few more times before I actually wholeheartedly embraced college. I had a colleague, Charles Casteel, who started at the company around the same time I did,

and our paths sort of tracked together as we progressed from our jobs as customer service representatives. By that time, I had jumped from an entry-level position to customer service to the director of several call centers with responsibility for more than 2,000 customer service representatives across nine states. One day, my coworker Charles said very casually, "Vic, you've stopped and started school so many times, if you had just taken one course each semester over these past 10 years, you would have had three degrees by now!" And guess what? He wasn't exaggerating. It really had been 10 years off and on. Ouch, that hurt then and I can remember feeling inwardly deflated. I certainly wasn't going to show an outward expression to affirm his comment. I had too much pride and attitude for that. Why couldn't he have used Zig Ziglar's encouraging words? "Put all excuses aside and remember this: YOU are capable." Geez!

Finally, one day while attending choir rehearsal at church, choir director Kathy Horry informed us that she would be graduating from the University of Maryland online program, UMUC. That was a new concept to me. Up until this point, all my on and off studies were on campus, sitting in a classroom with a professor lecturing in the front. Embarrassed that all these years later, I still didn't have my degree, I didn't join in the conversation about Kathy. I may have congratulated her, as I was sincerely happy about her accomplishment but I absolutely didn't want to get caught in a conversation about completing my degree.

Kathy must have picked up on the vibe and sure enough, she asked me when I would be done with school as she knew I had taken classes in years past. I was ready with my canned

excuse. I didn't have time with my demanding schedule, job responsibilities, heavy travel and caring for a husband and daughter. I figured, a degree just wasn't in the cards. In 30 seconds flat, she had the solution! Online learning was really starting to become very popular and by this time, students could actually complete their entire degree online.

I shot off another excuse that my learning style was to be sitting in a classroom on the front row, directly up under the teacher. I had convinced myself that I couldn't learn any other way. I explained to Kathy that if I got a "D" or lower that I would have to pay the company back. I shared with her that there was no way I could take a class online and actually pass it. Oh yeah, did I mention that my company paid for our schooling up to $8,000 annually? Actually, years prior when I was wasting time stopping and starting, it was unlimited tuition assistance. My company paid for the classes in advance and employees never had to come out of pocket unless we received the "D" letter grade or failed altogether. What in the world was I thinking??? Kathy ever so kindly encouraged me to sign up for the fall semester. She was on to all of my excuses, and she removed them. She said that if, for some strange reason, I received a "D" or failed, which she had no reason to believe that I would, she would pay my company back. My classes were $1500 each. This wasn't chump change; this was adult money.

Now what? I was without excuse. Recalling the words of the poem and the expression on Danielle's face as she recited it around the house, I enrolled in Strayer University's online program without hesitation hoping to secure a bachelor's

degree in business administration. This would certainly require some serious work-home-life balance given that I was married, mother of a teenager who happened to have her own crazy schedule between school, dance, basketball, and track! Part of the registration process was providing the transcript from my community college. I can remember going to the school, requesting it, paying for it, and laughing at myself the entire drive from the community college to the Strayer campus in Camp Springs, Maryland. Essentially, it was nearly pointless to get the transcript. I was starting from scratch. I think I was able to transfer no more than two classes worth of credits. The only class I didn't have to take at Strayer while getting my undergrad was accounting.

Lessons from the sidelines

Key lesson: Make every minute count, nothing's promised. While you don't need to strike the perfect balance; having some semblance of it is key.

I took up Amy Trask's game plan for finding the balance that worked for "6010" while I was pursuing my degree. While I was working on my bachelor's and subsequently MBA degree, all bets were off. Even before enrolling in school, I solicited the support of my husband, daughter, and other close family and friends, as it truly takes a village to keep all the balls in the air. With my demanding work schedule and constant travel, I knew I couldn't walk this journey alone. There were times that I may have needed my sisters to cook dinner for us, be at the house when the plumber arrived for repairs or even run to school and

pick up Danielle when she was ill because I just couldn't do it all, all at once. I needed the full support of everyone around me. I wanted to be sure that before I made such a huge personal and financial commitment, that my immediate family and responsibilities at work would not suffer. Once I got the green light from all involved, it was full steam ahead.

My discretionary time was slim to none. I can recall Sunday family dinners, most often hosted at my home, and while tons of laughter and fun were being had by all downstairs in the kitchen and family room, I was locked up in my office upstairs cranking out papers for three and sometimes four classes at a time. I will admit, four classes per semester as a full-time mom, wife, employee, community volunteer, not to mention non-stop travel for work was a bit insane, but I did what I had to do.

I will be the first to admit that this was not an easy process or journey. There were times when my daughter needed help as she was taking advanced courses in high school and I was trying to get my homework done. For a few semesters, probably more than I would care to admit, my family lived off cereal for dinner during the week and I was thrilled if I got more than four hours of sleep. The lack of sleep probably had a negative impact on me physically and emotionally. But I made a conscious effort to put on my game face at work. Although I hate to admit it, I took my family for granted at times and they experienced my crankiness more than anyone else. Depending on the travel schedule at work and school demands, there were days when I'm sure Troy and Danielle wished they didn't speak to me at all since I wasn't always too nice. I am truly grateful that, for the most part, they

didn't take it personal and knew I needed sleep and even on some occasions, food. I'm sure it wasn't funny then, but we certainly can laugh about it now that it's behind us. At times I didn't realize just how cranky I had become and they would dish it right back. And I would be the one with an attitude for having to put up with two cranks! Some nerve I had.

My last two semesters during my undergrad studies were the absolute worst. For some crazy reason, I thought it would be brilliant to take economics, logic, and math all at once. Surely, they all fit together so it would be like taking one big class, right? Absolutely not. A few weeks in, I was drowning, not eating, not sleeping and secretly crying crocodile tears whenever I was alone. I had too much pride to cry in front of anyone about school. One day, my middle sister, Dana, called and heard it in my voice. I think I actually had a meltdown on the phone and told her that I was calling up the school to quit. Who needs a degree anyway? I've worked hard and excelled to executive status without my bachelors degree, so why should I torture myself and neglect my family? At least in that vulnerable moment, that's how I saw it.

Being the great listener and most compassionate person on earth, she said, "Earth to Victoria, have you lost your mind! You are too close to quit. You will NOT quit. Hang up this phone, call the school ASAP and get a tutor. Do you hear me?"

Back in the game

Tears streaming down my face, I barely got out the word, "Yep."

I hung up the phone, still crying, even more dramatic now than when I was speaking to Dana, called Strayer and asked for a tutor. Within 24 hours, one was assigned and within 3 days, I was receiving tutoring from a professor on the Camp Springs campus.

I still couldn't make too much sense of economics, so on top of the school's tutor, I asked one of the kindest and smartest colleagues in finance, Jeff Gold, to help me and he did. (And even when Danielle was at Pepperdine University, enrolled in economics as a sophomore, she too struggled and the one and only Jeff Gold tutored her by phone all the way from Maryland. She got a "B.") Believe it or not, I did muster up the courage to finish and was more determined than ever to pass those classes. I ended up with a "B" in logic, an "A" in math, and a "C" in economics. At that point, I didn't care as long as I passed. I really thought those classes were going to wipe me off the face of the planet.

In between the last two semesters before finishing up the bachelors degree, I had an appointment for my annual physical. I had lost 20 lbs which for my height and build was not a good thing. My blood pressure was that of a 12-year-old and my doctor could not understand how I was even walking, let alone, keeping on top of my insane responsibilities at work and home. Dr. Wilson said in his calm voice, "I think you may want to consider taking a break after this semester. This unhealthy schedule of a few hours of sleep and not enough to eat won't last very long." He went on to remind me that if we don't take care of our natural bodies with adequate sleep, a healthy diet

and exercise, that the body will break down on us. Oh, by the way, I was still volunteering in the community because I had way too much pride and not enough wisdom to take a brief leave of absence. Although, I comprehended exactly what Dr. Wilson was saying, I was in such a trance and on auto pilot that, I dismissed his wise counsel and repeated the same dumb behaviors the next semester which fortunately, was the final semester. I just wanted to finish and be done with school for the moment.

Now that I look back, it wasn't such a great idea to take four classes during those last two semesters. But I was determined to get my bachelors by the end of my daughter's junior year in high school to ensure that she had the best senior year ever. I took her senior year off and enrolled in the MBA program the following year when she was a freshman in college. I figured by then, we would both benefit from us being in college at the same time. Some 18 months later, I finished the two-year MBA program. Upon completing my bachelor's and master's degrees, I reluctantly participated in the graduation ceremony. I just wanted my papers and had no desire to walk across the stage. Of course, my father would have something to say about this. He brought up the fact that Troy and I ran off to the justice of the peace to get married and robbed him of the opportunity to walk me down the aisle. Wow, Dad, lay on the guilt! Next, he reminded me that there were so many family members and friends who supported me on this journey, and he asked that I not rob them of the opportunity to see me walk across the stage. Who could argue with that?

Touchdown!

Not only did I walk both times, but I walked with honors and thankfully, my mom was alive to see it all. She got to see her constant words to me fulfilled: be a lifelong learner. No sooner than I graduated with honors from the MBA program, the school counselor called to advise me that I was four classes away from earning an executive graduate degree in Human Resources. I just couldn't get enough, so I signed up and took two classes over two semesters and walked away with those papers as well! On a side note, Troy and I renewed our wedding vows when we celebrated 20 years of marriage and had a full ceremony where my mom was present and my dad proudly walked me down the aisle!

As I reflect back on the days that I wanted to quit, not only did the poem about excuses keep flooding my mind but also the fact that this phase of life was only for a season. In my mind, how could I encourage my daughter to go to college and finish if I hadn't led by example? All I can say is that I am eternally grateful and thankful that I didn't quit, that I had folks all around me who kept me straight, and that God gave me the strength to finish and finish strong.

I think during this chapter of my life, I realized that sleep was overrated or at least that's what I told myself. At best, I would get 4-5 hours on any given night. To me, the sacrifice was worth the reward. You've heard it said that anything worth having is worth fighting for, and I've found that to be true. The biggest lesson and achievement for me during that time, in addition

to the degrees, was finding the peace that came with my own version of "balance".

"Happiness cannot be far behind a grateful heart and a peaceful mind."

– Unknown

Essentially, each of us must come to terms with our own balance, be grateful for those in our lives that support us, live life with no regrets, and be at peace with the outcome.

How will you find and define your balance today?

....

....

....

....

....

....

....

....

....

....

....

....

....

....

....

....

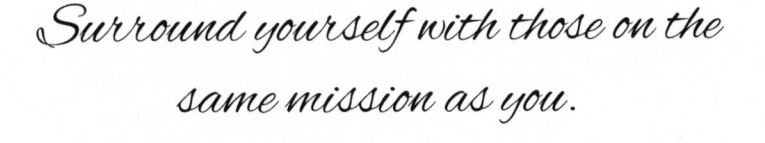

Surround yourself with those on the same mission as you.

Sleep is Overrated

Actor, Will Smith with an estimated net worth of more than $250 million said that he excels in having a ridiculous, sickening, work ethic. When others are sleeping and eating, and a few are out partying, he can be found working.

I've come to realize that we make time for whatever is important to us. Simply put, whatever is worth having, we have to work and sacrifice for it. When I started my career more than 28 years ago, I knew from watching my mom and dad's insane work ethic that I, too, had to put the work in. I never saw mom or dad napping, goofing off, or wasting one second on anything that didn't benefit their family. While they were not wealthy by today's standard or stacked with material things, the unconditional love provided daily and wisdom imparted to me was and is priceless. I never saw any unproductive time and most impressively, they taught me how to make the time good and to make every second count. I'm sure they goofed off and had fun and I'm sure they didn't always make every second count. However, my overall recollection of my childhood home was one of productivity.

As the youngest of seven children, I was taught at a very young age that responsibility, accountability, and work were not bad words. In fact, they were indeed, words to live by. I think I may have actually taken the word "work" a little bit too literal upon high school graduation as I had no desire at the time to go off to college even though that was the expectation in my home.

You see, I had been working every summer since reaching the legal working age of 14, in a coveted summer job with the DC government. I continued to work every day after school throughout high school. Even though I knew my parents were a little disappointed in my decision to continue working full-time post-high school rather than going directly to college like most of my friends and older siblings, they supported me every step of the way. A big part of this decision to work right out of high school was also driven by the fact that, not long after graduation, I learned that I was pregnant with Danielle. It would have been a huge challenge to attend college full-time, work full-time, and raise a newborn simultaneously. Even though I didn't take the traditional path like my parents had hoped, they reminded me daily, that I could achieve anything that I put my mind to and was willing to work for. I can recall my dad sharing his hopes of me attending Hampton University and if not college, joining the Air Force since I often joked about joining the military. My mom rarely sugar-coated anything and simply told me that this road would be tough. But after all, I was built for tough times, she said. The coaching they gave me was straightforward: get a plan, work the plan and realize that I was now a parent and every decision from that day forward needed to have my child and her wellbeing in mind. They always kept in front of me that sacrifice was a requirement and prerequisite to success.

It was in my early days that I realized that sleep was in fact overrated. I found myself much like Will Smith in that while my high school peers were napping after school, I was working. When they slept in on Saturday mornings, I was off to work! When they were hopping from house party to house party on a Friday night, I was studying. Failing wasn't an option and to be

able to attend high school and work full-time, I had to sacrifice something. Every so often I found time to go to a movie or attend the school dance, but the priority was to graduate with honors while working full-time, period. By having that Will Smith "sickening" work ethic in front of me all the days of my life by way of my parents, I was without excuse. As I continued to work full-time post high school, I realized that I had developed that sickening work ethic and made no apologies for it. I saw right off the break the incredible benefit and fruit it bore!

During my senior year in high school, I only needed two credits to graduate which afforded me a half-day schedule. I attended class in the morning and worked at the Department of Defense in the afternoons as part of the Washington, D.C., high school work program. Right after graduation, and even before I became pregnant, I was offered full-time employment with a step increase and promotion from a GS-2 to a GS-3. I thought I was big stuff and had convinced myself that I didn't need to worry about college. Not too long after accepting the Defense Department job, I learned that I was pregnant. So having the full-time job was perfect for us financially, in my mind. I think looking back, I allowed the pregnancy to convince me that I couldn't do both work and attend school with a new baby. In addition, my boyfriend (now husband) wasn't thrilled about raising a family in one of our parent's homes. Having a full-time job became my priority.

After Troy got over the initial shock that he was going to be a dad at the age of 23 and that he now would be responsible for just more than himself, our conversations began to shift

and focus on the three of us. I was very torn about the idea of moving. When Danielle was born, we were both still living in our respective parent's homes. My mom and dad were very helpful at night, especially since I had to get up early in the morning for work. We had created a nursery for my daughter in my parent's home and they had become very attached. Any time they heard us discussing moving out, tension would rise and sparks would fly. Troy and my dad had a great relationship; however, the relationship between Troy and my mom at that time was another story.

She wasn't too happy with the thought of us moving out to where she considered "so far away." The apartment we were considering was less than 30 minutes away. Troy was determined to find us our own place and be the man that he was created to be. He assured me that we would be okay in the process. We were both willing to make the sacrifices necessary, including missing a few hours of sleep, to make it work. Day care was at Troy's grandmother's house in DC, which meant I would be driving in rush-hour traffic to drop Danielle off, dash to work and frequently travel in peak traffic in the evenings to pick her up on days when Troy worked late. I will admit that, although it was very scary in the beginning, Troy was true to his word then and has been every day since.

Making sacrifices

Whether it's work, your family, or anything else deemed important to you, I would admonish you to give and deliver your very best self. Sacrifices will need to be made, there is no

side stepping.

I was raised to give my best and expected to be the best in everything I did, although that wasn't always the case. I was reminded from my parents, husband and even our pastor that I had purpose and others deserved my best self; it was just that simple. In order to walk in this, I had to make good choices.

Once again, I needed to make time for what was important. Having a demanding full-time job, being a wife and mom and at times, enrolled in school full-time, required incredible discipline and sacrifice. I quickly realized that sleep would be limited, but only for a season. Whenever I started a new job, took on a big project or needed to devote additional time to any area of my life, I found myself reminding my extended family and friends that during that particular season, I would have limited availability for things that didn't add true value to the cause, whatever the cause was at the moment. Essentially, the conversation would go something like this... "Hey guys, I've got papers to write and studying on tap, so please don't bother inviting me to the movies, parties, dinners, weddings or funerals for the next 18 months!" Of course, they knew I was sort of joking about the funeral comment, but I got the point across. I didn't have any discretionary time nor any energy to waste. I was about the business of producing best-in-class results at work, being there for my husband and daughter, doubling down to finish that degree, volunteering in the community or anything else that was important to me.

When I look back on the time that I accepted the challenge

from Kathy, the church choir director, to go back to school and to eliminate the excuses, I realize that I was building muscle memory needed to face subsequent challenges in my life. After accomplishing something that seemed a little out of reach, given all the balls I was juggling, the sacrifices made and sleep lost were certainly worth it!

What sacrifices are you willing to make today to achieve your goals?

....

....

....

....

....

....

....

....

....

....

....

....

....

....

....

....

....

....

....

....

....

"No alarm clock needed, my passion wakes me."

— Eric Thomas

3 Slow Nickels

The last time I checked, three slow nickels exceeded one quick dime any day of the week. Often times, I found myself going after the quick dime that wasn't sustainable nor fulfilling. As you see others around you getting new jobs, promotions or what seems to be exciting opportunities while your journey seemingly is taking a different and slower pace, it's hard to remember that three slow nickels always outpace one quick dime. The key to enjoying the journey is having patience and appreciation for every stage, every step, every turn, every detour, every setback, every comeback, every adversity, and every success experienced along the way.

The Chinese proverb, "Be not afraid of growing slowly, be afraid only of standing still" reminds me that all progress should be celebrated and that standing still is never an option. During my journey climbing the corporate ladder, I was frequently reminded by my mom, that my route may not be closely patterned after others and it's okay to make my own way. As a young, ambitious, passionate, energetic overachiever with the sincere desire to win and help others around me win, the quick dime always sounded good and the three slow nickels never made sense. Early in my career when I worked for the Department of Defense for three years, I was getting promoted every six months, which certainly built confidence. However, because of the quick moves, I wasn't able to learn from mistakes. By the time I realized my mistakes because I was already off to the next thing. When I moved on from the government to

the private sector in the summer of 1990, I was thrilled about the $10,000 jump in pay but the promotions weren't as fast as in the government. Still, I received several promotions in my new job and was leading employees twice as old as I was before the age of 25. What I didn't realize then but know now is that by moving around fast (hence the quick dime), I wasn't paying attention to mistakes, learning from them and making necessary adjustments along the way. It caught up with me later when I was leading larger, more complex teams.

During one of my quick-dime moves, I had the pleasure of working for one of the smartest men in the industry, the late Daniel Felder. He would call me into his office, and although I was his top sales account manager, he saw the gaps in my professional growth and maturity. Even though he saw that I was exceeding my goals and proud of my #1 status, he also saw, was that I wasn't spending enough time learning the financial aspects of the deals and developing overall business acumen. When he took the time to enlighten me, my career movement slowed some but I found that I was more effective. He taught me different approaches to inspire my team and peers to deliver results without leading by fear and intimidation. I was so busy focused on the next gig and motivated to nail the current job, I didn't realize that I came across as a bulldog. Thankfully, many of my colleagues knew my intentions but I can only imagine those who didn't really know me must have thought I was one crazy woman on a mission.

It wasn't until others who had traveled before me, achieved what I desired and filled with wisdom began to pour into my life

professionally and personally, that I realized the reward always accompanied the three slow nickels. Having the patience and perseverance to put the work in day in and day out when many around me did just enough to get by, started to pay off. I was able to focus on delivering best-in-class results with the ability to lap those results year after year versus chasing the next opportunity. Far too often, we can miss the incredible opportunities to learn, grow, develop, and stretch ourselves in the current position as a result of spending an inordinate amount of time running after the next big thing.

Take time to grow

I am a huge supporter of owning your own career, planning for it, charting the way, making the necessary connections and letting key stakeholders know what you want. But I am not a supporter of charting a career course that is paced so fast that you neglect your assignment or leave a trail of blood or cartilage behind. One wise person, my former director and now dear friend, Brenda Finch, once told me that it's mission critical to bloom where you're planted. In other words, do a great job in your current role, plan for the next move but do it in such a manner that it doesn't become a distraction or have a negative impact.

How are you currently blooming where you're planted?

....

....

....

....

....

....

....

....

....

What position do you currently have?

....

....

....

What position do you want?

....

....

....

What steps are you taking right now to make it a reality?

....

....

....

....

In what ways have you found yourself chasing the next big thing and putting yourself at risk for a quick dime that isn't sustainable versus securing three slow nickels?

....

....

....

....

James A. Garfield put it this way: "Be fit for more than the thing you are now doing. Let everyone know that you have a reserve in yourself; that you have more power than you are now using. If you are not too large for the place you occupy, you are too small for it."

———————————————⊗———————————————

"I've missed more than 9000 shots in my career. I've lost almost 300 games, 26 times I've been trusted to take the game winning shot and missed. I've failed over and over and over again in my life and that is why I succeed."

— Michael Jordan

———————————————⊗———————————————

Finish Strong

Photo: My parents in 2014, after 64 years of marriage. This is what commitment looks like.

Zig Ziglar reminds us, "Where you start is not as important as where you finish." You see, I used to be very insecure based on my starting point in my adult life. After all, I did not go off to college post-high school like most of my friends and siblings. In addition, my precious daughter was birthed out of wedlock. Certainly, my non-traditional start did not set me up for long-term success based on society's standards. Troy was 23 years old and I was 19. We experienced first-hand the challenges of raising a child at such a young age, including enduring the naysayers. There were many out there who had already written us off and told us that we wouldn't make it. I can remember primarily older co-workers who seemed to prejudge whether we could be successful as a family and essentially said, "This will never work."

The assumption was that Troy wouldn't step up to the plate, and we would become another statistic of a single mom and deadbeat dad with baby-mama drama. We were determined for that NOT to be our story. Funny enough, those who never believed in us are nowhere to be found and those family and close friends who cheered us on, coached us, prayed for us, and encouraged us every step of the way, remain in our lives today. You see, Troy worked full-time during the day and attended college classes in the evening. I figured I would just work full-time and not even try to attend school with everything that I was facing at the time.

My start wasn't so ideal and I had plenty of older adults frequently reminding me that to be successful in life, I should have attended college after high school, and should have waited until I was in my late twenties or thirties to get married and start a family. The way I saw it, I had two choices in front of me: I could either believe success wasn't an option based on my seemingly rocky start or believe that I could redirect my focus and energy and change the trajectory for my life.

Interestingly enough, there were always great examples in front of me and around me to show me what was possible, if only I was willing to change my perspective and see through different lenses.

My most favorite part of the working world was and still is, leading and inspiring others to achieve the impossible. Seeing the light bulbs go off in others is most energizing and rewarding. My own insecurities and self-doubt early in my career stemmed from the fact that most of my peers and leaders had college degrees and I didn't. Now I know first-hand the feeling when you achieve a goal you never thought possible. Deep down inside, I knew that I came from a family of champions and winners, but the negative thoughts that I allowed to roam free in my mind seemed to slow me down and sometimes had me off course. It wasn't until others around me, who saw something in me that I didn't see in myself, challenged me to walk in purpose and embrace my potential that my career took off. Even after several promotions, I made rookie mistakes like not being sensitive to the needs of my team and putting work and results first above everything else. Thankfully, by then, I was very open

to feedback and had a sincere desire to be better every day than the day before.

In order to finish something, you have to resolve in your mind and in your heart that it's worth the fight. Anything worth having is worth fighting for. For me, finishing is a mindset, it's a state of being. Mahatma Gandhi summed it up this way:

> "Your beliefs become your thoughts,
> Your thoughts become your words,
> Your words become your actions,
> Your actions become your habits,
> Your habits become your values,
> Your values become your destiny."

We all know that it's much easier to quit, but the nice thing is that when you get in the habit of finishing everything you start, no matter how big or small, you become a finisher in every aspect of your life.

I will tell you what I would frequently tell the new hires:

There will be some days that will be more challenging than others. There will be some customers that seem impossible to service. There will be co-workers that you honestly believe were sent on earth to make your day a living hell. There will be bosses that you will wonder, *how in the world did they ever make it into leadership?* I'm sure you can think of few to add to the list as well.

Find that person, place, or thing that drives you. Put a picture of this person, place or thing on the back side of your badge which you're likely to always have on in the office. Let this be a constant reminder of why you must finish. Let it remind you why it's imperative to finish and why quitting can never be an option. Let it remind you why you get out of bed day in and day out.

I always had a picture of my daughter on the back of my badge. It was the one thing that reminded me that no matter how tough things got or how hot the fire became, I had to finish so that she would have a chance at a better life. She never knew that her picture was on the back of my badge. I'm sure had she known it, she may have been mortified to know that her mommy carried a picture of her from age 1 until age 26. It was my constant reminder that I had to finish and finish strong.

Stay for the long-haul

I can honestly say that I didn't have to look very far for great examples of finishers. My husband's grandparents' 73-year marriage, finished strong. My mother- and father-in-law were married for 45 years before she passed. They finished strong. I realized that they were teaching everyone fortunate enough to be in their great company how important it is to finish and finish strong.

My parents were married 64 years before my mom passed Oct. 12, 2014, due to complications with dementia. Although her memory was still pretty sharp in the year leading up to her

passing, she was unable to really care for herself. I watched my dad, who has a bad back, lift my mom every morning and night as he bathed her, fed her, and got her out of bed and into her reclining chair. He never once complained. In fact, he looked forward to caring for her in such a meticulous way. We often reminded him that the nurse really did know what she was doing; it became our inside joke and the incredible nursing staff went along for the ride! He refused to leave her side and I am grateful that he was right there when she took her last breath. If up to that point I hadn't picked up on how to have a lasting relationship, watching my parents live out their vows – 'til death do us part — taught me more than I could ever learn about what commitment was really all about. I got a first-hand lesson on what it means to finish strong in marriage.

The key to all of their successful marriages was never quitting. Finish what you start!

Though I had great examples around me, I also didn't have to look very far for quitters and haters either. They absolutely made their presence known all day, every day. There will always be competing voices. The critical question is, which voice will you listen to? Which example will you follow? Will you be willing to put the work in to finish and finish strong?

When I announced my retirement after 25 years, I made sure that as I exited stage left, that I hung up my jersey as the #1 Area Vice President of Customer Service in the nation. In fact, I was the first African-American to ever serve in that position. It was a strong finish!

You see, I never thought any of this was possible based on my humble beginnings. As I celebrate 25 years of marriage and an incredible 25 year career, I look back with pride on achievements in my personal and professional life. I am especially proud of my daughter who finished college in three years and is now married and leading a non-profit organization with her husband, serving the youth of Compton (www.discoverYOUcompton.org). I can truly say, finishing strong pays big dividends!

At the beginning of this chapter, I quoted Zig Ziglar's reminder that where you start is not as important as where you finish. He also has pointed out, "Outstanding people have one thing in common: an absolute sense of mission."

How can you get laser-focused on your mission and busy finishing what you started today?

....

....

....

....

....

....

....

....

....

....

"It's kind of fun to do the impossible."

–Walt Disney

The Best is Yet to Come

Photo: Danielle and Dion Watson, expecting Baby Watson in june 2016.

As is customary with any team that I have had the privilege of serving, I make a commitment to invest in their leadership and professional development. In my last assignment before retiring, I was fortunate enough to have responsibility for more than 5,000 employees which included hundreds of supervisors and associate directors in addition to my direct reports which also consisted of 11 directors and an executive assistant.

Each year I, along with a few of my support staff, would review my vision for the annual leadership summit and all the associated moving parts. It was a huge undertaking as my team was spread out from Maine to Alabama. It wasn't always easy to bring the leaders to a central location for a few days of development and in some cases we did just that and in other times, we suitcased the summit and took it on the road to each of the locations.

For the Spring 2015 leadership summits, we packaged a robust agenda with incredibly talented, experienced and brilliant speakers who were all members of my leadership team and hit the road! It was two full weeks of back-to-back travel up and down the east coast with the team; I enjoyed every minute. We spent several hours in the car driving from one location to the next and we learned a great deal from one another. This was one of my most favorite times of the year. This time, I asked one of my managers to present on a topic, and while she was delighted for the opportunity, the timing wasn't the best as she was caring for a sick parent at the time. However, as any responsible

leader would do, she didn't leave me hanging. In fact, she recommended one of her peers to present on a very hot topic: employee engagement. This was perfect on so many fronts. For starters, her peer was a newer manager within the organization and had a very critical role. She was responsible for ensuring my organization's attendance was best-in-class, that employee attrition lowered and overall employee satisfaction improved as well as helping drive meaningful employee engagement in general.

I think anyone would agree that her role was essential to our team's success. It was a no-brainer to have this new manager hit the road with us and become one of the leadership summit presenters. While her presentation and call to action regarding employee engagement was a big hit, and the managers in attendance at the summits took away actionable best practices that they could immediately implement to improve results, she was also a hit during the leadership panel discussion that I had the pleasure of moderating.

The topic of making gutsy moves in our careers came up in every one of our leadership panel discussions. I moderated the panel and along with the attendees was super-charged by each of the leadership discussions. There was one question the new manager posed to the audience at every summit: What would you do if you were not afraid? Every time that question was raised, I thought to myself, *Wow, that's a great question for the audience!* I got super excited each time and couldn't wait to hear the responses from the audience. A few leaders said they would take on different jobs that required them to relocate their

families if they were not afraid. Others said they would go back to school and complete their degrees, start their own business, etc. Although I was fascinated by the question and responses, I never entertained the question for myself.

What if I wasn't afraid?

Months later, I watched my daughter and son-in-law pour their heart and soul into their non-profit — Discover YOU Compton, Inc. They have paused very successful professional dancing and acting careers to launch their social justice, arts and education non-profit. And that's when I realized, working on behalf of our youth is something I would do if I were not afraid to leave my comfortable, familiar, seemingly secure, and overall successful 25-year career at Verizon.

And so it came to be that in July 2015, an opportunity presented itself where I could, in fact, retire after 25 amazing years at what I believed was the best company in the entire world. After all, this career afforded me so many opportunities to care for my immediate and extended family in ways I never thought possible. Why in the world would I ever consider another option?

So here I am, doing exactly the things that I was afraid to do: writing my first book, supporting my daughter's non-profit full time, continuing to serve on the National Network to End Domestic Violence board, volunteering in the community, helping young leaders get established and spending precious time with my family.

Whatever stage of life you are in, wherever you are in your professional career, understand that the best is always to come. Appreciate where you are now, but know that it's a journey. While the phases of my life that I shared throughout this book are mostly behind me, there's still more life ahead of me. I encourage you to embrace your future just as I'm doing. You may reach a point or have already reached a point where you need to answer the same question that I found myself answering not too long ago: *What would I do if I were not afraid?* If you're like me, analytical and detailed oriented, you may want all the details laid out as the unknown can be frightening. Now that I'm actively in what I would describe as Act II of my life, the unknown is still somewhat scary but the hope that I have reminds me, "It's all good." You, too, may be at a crossroads in your life. Well, stop stressing and enjoy the journey! The Second Act may be your best one yet.

I will admit that I am not exactly sure of how my Second Act will develop, or the array of professional opportunities that will arise. However, what I am well assured of is the very fact that the best is yet to come for me and you!

What would you do if you weren't afraid? What's holding you back? It's time to journal and face your fears head-on so that you too will overcome them.

....

....

....

....

....

....

....

....

....

....

....

....

"You can't start the next chapter of your life if you keep re-reading the last one."

Photo: My dad and I. #ageisjustanumber

Acknowledgments

My dad, Ellsworth Hutchinson, Jr. — you knew all along that I had a book on the inside of me and you are the one who inspired me to pause and share my story so that I may inspire others! Thank YOU!

My sisters, Donna Marshall and Dana McCoy — you pushed me, encouraged me and cheered me on along the way. Nothing like sisters!

My nephew and niece, Ryan and Sara Hutchinson — you stayed up with me for two nights in a row brainstorming the title! I sure do appreciate you guys!

My middle brother, David Hutchinson, the private investigator — you kept me on track by calling periodically to interrogate me. Love you lots!

My oldest brother, Ronald Hutchinson — surprise! I kept this a secret from you! Sorry!

My amazing in-laws and other nephews and nieces, Lisa Hutchinson, Shellye Hutchinson, Lawrence Marshall, Robert Murray III, Josh and Lauren Coyle, Aaron and Jasmine Ray, and Brittany Hutchinson — you continue to be my raving fans. Love you to the moon and back!

Mark & Bea Dabney and Clint & Yodi Crouch – the best cousins and friends $$$$ could buy!

My incredible daughter, Danielle Jai (Boston) Watson and selfless son-in-law, Dion Watson — you call me your hero, but you haven't quite realized yet, that you are in fact my heroes! Unlimited hugs & kisses!

My best friend, lover, confidant, life partner, father of my amazing daughter, my personal comedian and husband of 25 incredible years, Troy Pernell Boston — you are the reason I wake up every day and give my very best self to the world in which we live. Endless love – xoxoxoxoxo!

Special thanks to all who have poured into my life both professionally and personally. I had three extra special bosses who were divinely placed in my life at various stages — almost strategically:

Brenda Finch, my first customer service and sales director back in the 90s. You didn't pull any punches. I am so grateful that you and I remain close and often laugh about the time that you said to me, after I repeatedly brought problems about the work environment to your attention... "Vicky, since you have so much mouth, so much to say and can point out all the problems, how about you get into a leadership position and help affect change." In less than six months, I was promoted into management.

Eric Cevis, you were vice president of large business internet sales at the time that I convinced myself that I wasn't cut out for the

corporate account executive sales position in your organization. I let you know, 30 days after accepting the promotion, I was going to retreat back to my previous position where I was very comfortable. You came from behind your desk, sat right next to me at the round table in his office and said… "No Vicky, you are not going to go back to your old position. That would mean that you are quitting and winners don't quit." I thanked you for your time, returned to my office, got out of my feelings, asked my peers for help and finished that year #1 in the nation as the 1st African-American female internet sales account manager. Thank you for believing in me.

Andrea Custis, my Vice President before retiring in 2011 — you had a real appreciation for my talent, tenacity, natural ability to lead and inspire. Your real desire to get the best out of others, pushed me far beyond what I ever thought possible. You constantly reminded me that… "Vicky, you were built for this, there's no one better" and you inspired me to go hard every day and most importantly, to finish strong.

Matt Patterson — for sharing your incredibly inspiring story, *My Emily,* with me that put me in high gear.

My coach, Jonathan Sprinkles — for reminding me that "It CAN Be Done."

Delina Pryce McPhaull — for keeping me on my toes throughout the entire publishing process. Amazing!

Gratitude changes everything. I am forever grateful.

About the Author

Victoria L. Boston currently serves as the Director of Community Relations for Discover YOU Compton Inc., a social justice non-profit organization bringing arts and education to underserved youth in Compton, CA.

Boston has nearly 30 years of corporate and community leadership experience with proven success at every stage of the game. Her energy and passion to connect others to what's

possible is unmatched. She holds an MBA in Marketing, Bachelors in Business, Executive Graduate degree in Human Resources, Project Management Certificate; has countless hours of executive leadership development from Columbia University Graduate School of Business and is a graduate of the Master Series for Distinguished Leaders in Washington, D.C. Coupled with firsthand experience, she delights to share her keys to success with others. The road Boston has traveled is full of lessons learned from mistakes made, setbacks and comebacks, and is loaded with priceless, yet timeless nuggets to help others reach their potential as they travel on their own journey.

An inspirational leader, author, speaker, coach, and community volunteer, she has the natural ability to influence and inspire greatness in those she encounters. Boston has the unique gift of connecting with diverse audiences, displaying total transparency while remaining authentic. She has electrified so many across the country ranging from elementary school students, colleges, churches, nonprofit organizations and in corporate settings for intimate groups with as few as 10 and as large as 20,000 attendees of all ages at the Mercedes Benz Superdome in New Orleans, LA.

A humble recipient of many honors, she has been awarded the prestigious Verizon CEO Leadership Excellence Award for exceptional results, the National Diversity Award, and the Dr. Martin Luther King, Jr. Leadership Award for her commitment to the professional development of others. In addition, she received a Certificate of Appreciation from the United States Department of Agriculture for her significant contributions

to their EEOAC Women's History Month celebration, was the keynote speaker at the University of North Carolina Wilmington College, Office of Institutional Diversity and Inclusion annual conference. She has been a three-time guest speaker at Strayer University for the school of business as well as a keynote speaker at a Strayer commencement ceremony. Recognized for her outstanding support of the Maryland Business Roundtable for Education Achievement Counts Program, Boston has been a guest speaker on multiple occasions at the Francis Scott Key Middle School's Career Day, and twice acknowledged for her leadership from Michelle Ebanks, President of Essence Communications. Celebrated as Verizon's Women "Making History Now" campaign and "Don't Just Celebrate History, Create It" black history month honoree, she has also been featured twice for her contributions in the local community in the Baltimore Afro American newspaper in which her late maternal grandmother, Constance Eleanor Daniel was one of the first African-American female journalists.

Boston is an active member at her local church, From the Heart Church Ministries in Suitland, MD, and serves on the Board of Directors for Discover YOU Compton Inc. in Compton, CA, the National Network to End Domestic Violence (NNEDV) and The Skills Society Foundation in Washington, D.C.

KEEP IN TOUCH
I WOULD LOVE TO HEAR FROM YOU!

f Victoria Boston

🇮 BostonVictoria

🐦 @vboston222

in bostonvictoria

www.VictoriaBoston.com